Peter Morea graduated in psychology at University College, London. In 1965 he obtained an M.A. in occupational psychology at Birkbeck College while working in the civil service and industry. He worked first in careers guidance and then in personnel and training. He subsequently joined Middlesex Polytechnic, where he was a principal lecturer in the School of Psychology until 1990. His main areas of academic interest are personality and philosophy. He has previously published *Guidance, Selection, and Training*, a textbook in occupational psychology. He is married and has grown-up children.

Peter Morea

PERSONALITY

An Introduction to the Theories of Psychology

PENGUIN BOOKS

PENGUIN BOOKS

Published by the Penguin Group
Penguin Books Ltd, 27 Wrights Lane, London W8 5TZ, England
Penguin Books USA Inc., 375 Hudson Street, New York, New York 10014, USA
Penguin Books Australia Ltd, Ringwood, Victoria, Australia
Penguin Books Canada Ltd, 10 Alcorn Avenue, Toronto, Ontario, Canada M4V 3B2
Penguin Books (NZ) Ltd, 182–190 Wairau Road, Auckland 10, New Zealand

Penguin Books Ltd, Registered Offices: Harmondsworth, Middlesex, England

First published 1990
3 5 7 9 10 8 6 4 2

Printed in England by Clays Ltd, St Ives plc
Filmset in 10/12 pt Monophoto Plantin

CONTENTS

For Sally

INTRODUCTION

You may think that there are important differences between you and an ape, such as being able to speak and make machines and know right from wrong, and say your prayers, and other little matters; but that is just a child's fancy, my dear.

Charles Kingsley: *The Water Babies*

Yes, this thing we call personality is a great and mysterious problem. Everything that can be said about it is curiously unsatisfactory and inadequate . . .

Jung: *The Development of Personality*

The science of personality began, conveniently, with the century when in 1900 Freud published *The Interpretation of Dreams*. In spite of his warning that 'None of us are adult till we stand by our father's grave,' Freud's psycho-analytic children have refused to bury him. Fifty years after his death psychologists, psychiatrists and feminists still stand about the coffin arguing. Whatever they finally agree as the testament he bequeathed to us, because of Freud we will never see ourselves in the same way again. This is what any good theory of personality does – it changes the way we see ourselves. This book outlines six such theories from modern psychology.

Freud, though not a believer, was proud of his Jewish heritage. Jewish humour is often a form of spirituality, attempting to deflate human arrogance, and Freud himself was pleased to prick this bubble of pride. The process had begun earlier when Copernicus realized that the Earth went round the Sun. Human beings were no longer situated in the middle of the universe and could not continue seeing themselves at the centre. With Darwin and evolution the humiliation went further when it became clear that we were first cousins to the ape. As part of the animal kingdom we could no longer regard ourselves as unique, even on Earth. But human beings still appeared to be special: they were full of high motives; they were rational; their lives and civilizations were shaped by right and wrong. Freud believed that he had exploded this last myth. If humans have higher motives, they have lower ones too – they are not particularly rational, and their everyday actions are governed by sex, aggression and unconscious forces. Human society resembles a Darwinian jungle where only the fittest survive.

If Freud is the father of personality theory, Skinner is a founding father of behaviourism. No amount of criticism has managed until now to dislodge behaviourism from centre-stage in modern psychology; cognitive psychology is now doing so. Skinner realized early on that Pavlov's work with dogs was important for understanding humans and proceeded to train animals to a level that is quite without equal outside a circus. People in the ordinary sense do not exist; we are simply creatures of habit, formed by pleasure and pain. Hamlet's 'How like a God!' may be poetic but 'How like a pigeon!' is nearer the scientific truth. When Skinner published *Walden Two*, a novel about a utopia based on the conditioning of behaviour, he angered and frightened many readers. Critics were not sure whether the novel was intended to be taken seriously or as satire; Skinner meant it seriously. His account of human beings remains in a sense the most scientific of our theories and difficult to dismiss, but it is the one that most contradicts common sense.

Our third thinker is Carl Rogers, an elder statesman of humanistic psychology, whose new thinking provided an alternative to psycho-analysis and behaviourism. His differences with behaviourism led to an inconclusive series of public debates with Skinner. Rogers had found in psychotherapy how important for his clients was a sense of their own self; Shakespeare's advice, 'To thine own self be true', appeared sound. But behaviourists had already dismissed the self as fiction and scientific nonsense. Rogers, trusting what his clients told him, put the self back into personality. His positive views contrast with

Freud's pessimism and have made more optimistic the thinking of therapists, teachers and marriage counsellors. They have even influenced hippies. Rogers made us aware how much we long for fulfilment and he offered hope of the good life. If men and women today walk out on their marriage because they do not find the relationship fulfilling, Rogers must take some of the credit – and blame.

Having circled the trinity of psycho-analysis, behaviourism and humanistic psychology, we make the trip a second time, starting with Freud's squabbling heirs, the neo-Freudians. Erich Fromm was an important neo-Freudian and, influenced by Marx, he saw that Freud's account of personality ignored society. Realizing that Marx in his turn had ignored personality in his account of society, Fromm caused more argument among the neo-Freudians by attempting to integrate the two. His graceful prose is widely read as a remarkable *tour de force* that goes beyond putting Freud into society and giving Marxism a human face, to incorporate history, philosophy, sociology and religion. In his account of the twentieth century we recognize our own condition as individuals lost in big organizations, economic playthings at the mercy of capitalism, alienated citizens haunted by the menace of totalitarian governments. The young, in particular, read Fromm to see what meaning they can extract for their lives in a godless universe.

The social behaviourism of role theory and George Herbert Mead appeals to sociologists, the political Left and feminists. The approach reveals how class, race and gender shape and constrain our lives. These and other roles determine success at school, our jobs, our health, our wealth and whether or not we end up as criminals, bigots or mentally ill. The roles we fill not only decide our chances in life but also form our personalities. Mead does not leave people completely at the mercy of circumstances, but any account which stresses that our fortunate situation in life is not due to innate talent and is largely the result of chance is disliked by the political Right. Whatever genetics and biology eventually discover about inborn human differences, the social behaviourist approach will never be redundant. The knowledge that all the world's a stage will remain an invaluable insight, relevant to our understanding of personality.

The final theorist, unknown to the general public, has considerable influence in psychology and one that is increasing. At international conferences, lectures are continually being given on George Kelly's construct theory, and books using Kelly's ideas appear yearly. In line with psychology's recent emphasis on the cognitive, on thinking and remembering and learning, Kelly put mind back into personality. Reacting against Freud's stress on bodies and biology and Skinner's view that the human organism is empty, Kelly said that what matters is mind and that human beings are mind-full. As a clinical practitioner he never separated psychological theory from practice and its application as a healing science. As a humanistic psychologist he emphasized that when we study personality what we study is ourselves. If a physicist looks at particles, the particles do not look back at the physicist; the human subjects that the psychologist studies *do* stare back. Kelly was keenly aware it is not just the psychologist who is scientific; the human subjects staring back are as much scientists as the men and women in white coats who are studying them.

As a psychologist I am puzzled by these odd creatures that we are. As a human being I feel, as Shakespeare's Miranda does, wonder before them and the world they have created – 'O brave new world,/That has such people in't!'. The students I teach expect that where literature evokes wonder, science will provide explanation. But personality seems wider and deeper than any theory can capture. Certainly our six theories leave unsolved problems that have always troubled philosophers. They fail to account for our minds and how they relate to our bodies. They fail to decide whether we are free and freely choose what we do or whether our acts are caused, like a gate blown open by the wind. They fail to explain if human beings are moral and if we are born good or bad. And our six theories sometimes exaggerate half-truths at the expense of common sense. The contribution of common sense to our understanding of personality has been neglected, and our theories often supplement, but do not supplant, common sense. Sometimes our theories contradict common sense; sometimes they contradict each other.

Human beings remain a puzzle in spite of the revealing perspectives and the wealth of knowledge and insight that psychology provides. Theories of personality do not explain human beings – nothing does that completely. Like literature and art, what personality theory does, as much as gives understanding, is to evoke wonder and the experience of mystery.

Many colleagues at Middlesex Polytechnic have helped with this book. I have discussed much with them, and they have read and commented on chapters. One would normally thank them by mentioning their names. But some, disagreeing with the arguments of the book or embarrassed by its conclusions, may not wish to be publicly associated with it, so I have expressed my gratitude to each personally, and I thank them without naming them here.

Chapter One

THE PUZZLE

Personality is the supreme realization of the innate idiosyncrasy of a living being. It is an act of high courage flung in the face of life, the absolute affirmation of all that constitutes the individual . . .

Jung: *The Development of Personality*

It has been fashionable for some time to debunk human beings. Putting people down began as a healthy reaction against the belief of the Victorians that human beings were rational, were good and were getting better. Such optimism was part of the imperial spirit of the age. But the new theory of evolution, later used to debunk human beings, was also responsible for the optimism. In evolution higher and superior species emerge, and things generally improve. If it happens in evolution, it would happen in human life.

But the idea of evolution eventually started the debunking process. Since we are first cousins to the ape, it has suited scientists to emphasize our animal nature as some sort of proof of evolution. This has led to the fashionable emphasis on the zoological side of men and women. We are naked apes, hunters in packs, tool-using primates, animals with selfish genes and territorial imperatives and drives to dominate. Human behaviour is governed by instinct and the evolutionary past; our bodies decide our destiny. If a middle-aged man leaves his middle-aged wife for a younger woman, his genes are to blame; it was no choice of his. As a consequence of millions of years of evolution his body is instructed by biology to maximize the chances of the human race surviving. His body reacts more strongly to the firmer breasts, smoother skin, more nubile shape of the younger woman. His body knows that any of its sperm

7

is more likely to produce offspring with her than with his ageing wife. She should not take it personally!

Equally fashionable in academic circles is the contrasting view that minds are important, not bodies. Human beings are computers. In an attempt to be scientific, psychology adopts ideas from contemporary technology. For Freud, personality resembled the hydraulic systems that were important in the engineering of his day. When I was a student, psychologists likened human beings to a telephone exchange. The current technology is the computer, so, of course, computers are what we are! As computers, we solve problems using the usual hardware of brain and memory for processing and storing information. We have input-output equipment of eyes, ears and hands. We learn, think, calculate, create, behave because we are equipped with a variety of programs, the equivalent of ... mind? Or is mind the programmer? This is where it begins to get tricky. But computers or information-processing systems are what we are, which explains why we act in the way we do. In mental illness information is coded and processed incorrectly, and treatment eliminates bugs in the system and reprograms the patient.

These two fashionable views of humans, as naked apes and as living computers, are a version of the age-old split into body and mind, heart and head, emotion and intellect. The naked ape and computer accounts dispel any mystery, as they are intended to. But somewhere in between is the creature that fills Miranda and most of us with wonder, and somewhere in between is an area occupied by common sense. It is time, with the help of common sense and personality psychology, to debunk the debunkers.

Common sense is an awareness of obvious truths, a knowledge of what is self-evident and unavoidable. To disprove the idea that matter did not exist Dr Johnson kicked a large stone – 'I refute it *thus*.' This is common sense at work. And when it comes to human personality, common sense has privileged access and inside information.

But common sense is a changing body of knowledge and is sometimes wrong. It was once obvious that the Sun went round the Earth – you had only to use your eyes. Now it is common knowledge that the Sun does not go round the Earth and that the Earth is not flat. Common sense changes and develops, and there is an interaction between common sense and the growth of knowledge. New academic ideas impinge on common sense, which absorbs some of them and rightly leaves others on the sidelines. The idea of an unconscious, of thoughts out of awareness that affect what we do, is now part of an informed common sense. But the idea of phrenology, that people's characters can be known from the shape of their skulls, is not.

The contribution of an informed and enlightened common sense is invaluable. In everyday life we constantly adopt common-sense explanations of human behaviour, and common sense is at its best with human behaviour. As we have said, when it comes to personality we have inside knowledge from personal experience. 'She married him because she wanted children' is common sense. The psycho-analytic 'She married him because (unknown to herself) he reminded her of her father' supplements but does not supplant the common-sense explanation. The scientific may add to the common-sense account without making it redundant. Humans have many motives (and causes) for what they do. 'He applied for the head-of-department job because he was ambitious' is common sense again. More scientific is 'His application was caused by an innate drive to be leader of the pack.' But the zoological explanation adds very little and is likely to remain on the sidelines of thought.

It is difficult to study human beings scientifically, since we are studying ourselves. If we stand far off and study humans objectively as just a species of animal or a special kind of computer, the perspectives are distant and unreal. But this is the kind of explanation that current fashion adopts – as if it were unscientific to look at human beings as human beings! We should not take too seriously statements about human beings made by biological and computer-inclined scientists. Saying that a human being is a naked ape or an information-processing computer tells us very little. Our common sense knows that being human is nothing like being an ape or a computer.

9

Psychological theories of personality are better placed. They are able to stand back and be scientific, but they are not so distant as to remain beyond the reach and criticism of common sense.

If we stand back, but not too far, what we notice about humans is their strangeness. What makes them strange is not the big breasts or large penis, the absence of much hair on their chests or anywhere else, the long period of growth and dependency, or their memory store and their brain's capacity to process information. What makes human beings strange and different is language, culture, art, morals, religion, law, technology, science, a complicated social life and an intense need for love and relationships. They talk, think, dance, sing, read, believe, get neurotic, feel guilt, build societies that survive them and civilizations that they are not happy with and tend the graves of their dead. All of this odd behaviour is the product of personality. Human beings are part of the living world; they recognize a kinship with other animals but know they are different. They are part of nature but apart from nature in a way that dogs and chimpanzees are not; neither dog nor chimp is ever likely to consider the matter. The human world is not particularly good: it includes warfare, holocausts, torture, exploitation, slavery, rape, and an endless list of other brutalities. We could certainly say, 'Man is a wolf to man,' except that this would be unfair to wolves – no wolf behaves so badly. The debunking of human beings is misleading and needs to be stopped, not because humans are good or better than other animals but because they are different.

What is this odd creature we see a specimen of every time we look in the mirror? In the following pages we consider three traditions that have made up the unholy trinity of personality theory: Freudian and neo-Freudian, behaviourist and social behaviourist, and the humanistic. In psychology there is no shortage of excellent theories of personality. We could add many others such as trait and factor theories, those of Jung, Adler and Eysenck, social learning, object relations and other neo-Freudian accounts. There are almost too many explanations, and the best criticism of each of our six theories often comes from the other five. They sometimes contradict one another. It is strange that there should be such a variety of good theories, and this has prompted students to ask, 'But which one is right?' I reply, 'Perhaps they all are.' There are many perspectives to personality. Men and women are (in the nicest possible sense) many-faced, and personality seems bigger than any one theory can capture.

The theories we outline tell us much more about human beings than any comparison with naked apes or computers can. But what should a good theory of personality explain? The Bible begins with Adam and Eve losing their innocence in the Garden when they choose to eat the fruit from the forbidden tree. The myth is suggesting that humans are free. The myth also suggests how like a god they become in knowing right from wrong and in having minds, just as the serpent promised: 'In the day you eat from the tree, your eyes shall be opened and you shall be like God, knowing both good and evil.' Any adequate explanation of personality must confront these three age-old puzzles: free will, morality and mind.

First, free will. Hamlet asks, 'To be or not to be' but is he really in a position to choose? Is he really free, as he seems to think, or is his behaviour and everyone else's *caused*? We live in a universe where the actions of everything else are caused, so why should human beings be an exception? In the night the gate bangs because of the wind, and I lie awake deciding whether to get up and close it. The wind that makes the gate bang is caused by differences in air density, which are caused by variations in heat on the Earth's surface, which are caused by the heat of the Sun, which is caused by ... An unbroken chain of cause and effect always exists. Is what I do when I get up and close the gate or turn over and go back to sleep another link in that chain of cause and effect? Or are human beings free? If free human behaviour exists, it really is a rarity since cause and effect clearly characterize our corner of the universe.

Next, morality. Were aliens to arrive from another planet, we might make them welcome – but would they want to stay? A glance at the papers and they would quickly realize that a lot of nasty and dangerous things are going on, and this might precipitate a quick getaway. Apart from shopping lists, our oldest surviving documents are accounts of wars. Human beings do seem to have eaten of the Tree of the Knowledge of Good and Evil. A theory of personality would have to account for wars, violence, exploitation, torture, murder, rape and the general brutality that characterize human existence. The original sin of the Adam and Eve story suggests the existence of some inborn inclination to evil in human beings. Another view, popular with the political Left, is that humans are born either good or blank slates, and aggression, murder, rape and the rest are something we learn. Certainly there is much good, and the Gandhis and Mother Teresas of this world to account for, as well as the Stalins and Hitlers and the evil. Perhaps evil is just a disease: what the Hitlers and rapists need is not punishment but treatment or retraining, like a dog that bites the postman. All societies have an idea of good and bad; from an early age children exclaim, 'That's not fair,' appealing to a sense of right and wrong which they believe their parents share. Most humans are aware of 'ought' and 'ought not': 'I ought not to have hit her, though she provoked me.' What is this still, small voice of conscience which distinguishes right from wrong and tells us what we should and should not do? Herd instinct? A social contract? Or is there some moral law written into men and women?

Finally, any theory must show what mind is, even whether it exists or is illusion. If mind is illusion, it remains a remarkably persistent one that will not go away. If mind does exist, what is it made of and how does it relate to body? My body has a virus that makes me feel depressed, and reading a book cheers me up. Body affects mind, and mind affects body. Today we are more than ever aware of the extent to which body and mind affect each other: drugs working on the body relieve states of mind such as anxiety and depression; anxiety, depression and tension cause ulcers and high blood pressure. What is this mind that feels depressed, cheers up, thinks, remembers and – if we are free – decides and chooses? Does it relate to body like a spirit in a machine? Since ancient times, food and the necessities for a journey have been left at gravesides and are evidence of belief in something – call it spirit – surviving the body's death. But science says that spirit does not exist and that body and mind are the same; both are matter, claims science. What is clear is the difference mind makes, the difference between being awake and being unconscious, fainted away, under anaesthetic, asleep, blind drunk. But if mind exists, it is remarkably rare: like free will, there is little of it about in our corner of the universe, and humans have most of what there is.

A watchmaker takes a clock to bits and lays out its parts on the table. He can point to the mechanisms, say what each is for and show how they all fit together for it to work. We need a theory of personality which, like the watchmaker, can explain what makes us tick: it would tell us what we are, why we are the way we are, and would explain how we change in some respects, stay the same in others, and why people are different. And a comprehensive psychology of personality would account for free will, morality and mind.

Personality psychology has more to tell us than any naked ape or computer accounts, but it has its limitations too. When I lecture on Freud and other established theories, I find myself facing students, both young and mature, who expect a revelation to unbind their eyes and make all things clear. I think of the health warnings carried on the cigarette advertisements and long to start the lecture with a similar caution: 'This lecture carries a common-sense warning – it may lead you to think that we understand human beings, but we don't.' My lecture does not explain personality and nor does any theory. My earlier answer to the students' query as to which theory is right – 'Perhaps they all are' – was a half-truth; common sense tells me that they are all inadequate.

Psychologists often despise common sense. Common sense tells us that we love our parents, but psycho-analytic probing of the unconscious reveals that we often hate them as well. But before any probing of the unconscious took place, there was already some common-sense awareness that our feelings for our parents were mixed. The stories of Oedipus and Hamlet could not have been written without this awareness. Psycho-analysis brought this knowledge into the light of day, revealing just how mixed our feelings are; and this has now become part of an informed common sense. Scientific theories provide unique points of view, which supplement and sometimes shape our common-sense understanding of ourselves; at other times they contradict common sense. But with or without the help of common sense, scientific theories do not explain personality; they do not make our experience of ourselves understandable. They do not do what the watchmaker does with a clock: strip down the parts, reassemble them and show what makes the whole thing tick. The clock must yield to the watchmaker's skill, but personality will always defeat the attempts of Freud, Skinner, Rogers and others to explain human beings. But, as we shall argue in the final chapter, in this failure an invaluable insight into personality is gained and – more importantly – a unique experience.

Human beings have always found that they are a mystery to themselves – 'Thrown into the world I become a puzzle to myself,' said St Augustine. The scientific study of psychology has added immensely to our knowledge and intellectual insight; and our six theories present revealing perspectives on personality. But we need to recover the wonder Miranda felt before human beings, and theories of personality make this possible.

Chapter Two

THE SAVAGE INFANT:
Freud's psycho-analysis

Nature, red in tooth and claw . . .

Tennyson: *In Memoriam*

Herr Schmidt is having an affair with the wife of his best friend. The friend is seriously ill and Herr Schmidt intends to marry the wife as soon as the husband dies. Recently the husband made a remark which seemed to hint that he knew about the affair and, shortly afterwards, Herr Schmidt had a disturbing dream. He dreamt he was having an affair with a woman someone else wanted to marry, but he was worried that the other man might find out and this would stop the marriage. In the dream Herr Schmidt kisses and embraces the other man.

What the dream is about appears to be obvious since it resembles Schmidt's real-life situation. But for Freud the key to dreams is not to be found externally but inside, in the unconscious they reveal. In Freud's view the dream is about when Herr Schmidt was a little boy – not that he has changed much since! Why, in a Vienna of eligible single women, does Herr Schmidt *choose* to fall in love with the woman married to his best friend? But he does not choose. The married woman he falls in love with, both in the dream and in real life, is the woman he never fell out of love with, his mother. The best friend she is married to is the man he has loved (and hated) all his life, his father. Herr Schmidt is still in love with his mother and still hates the rival for his mother's affections, his father. His present fears about the husband's suspicions echo his child-hood terror that Father would find out about his feelings for Mother. As a child he had often wished his father dead, and

15

now in phantasy that wish is about to come true. His best friend, married to the woman he loves, is dying. In the dream Herr Schmidt masks his hostility by kissing and embracing him. According to Freud, in *The Interpretation of Dreams*, what this dream reveals is an oedipus complex.

And it will not end there, the dream tells us. Should nothing come of the affair, Herr Schmidt will not turn over a new leaf and start looking among single women for a suitable sexual partner. He will stick to women who are married, like his mother. Both the real-life affair and the dream are caused by that unsolved oedipus conflict of childhood. All men either get stuck in their oedipus stage, like Herr Schmidt, or scrape through to end up like their fathers and marry women like their mothers. In Freud's view, we live in the past and adult life is only a re-run of childhood. As George Russell (A. E.) wrote in his poem 'Germinal': 'In the lost boyhood of Judas/Christ was betrayed.' What happens to us as children fixes our adult personality. It may be obvious in the case of a man who marries a woman old enough to be his mother, or in that of a wife who cannot bring herself to leave the husband who beats her up, just as her father beat her mother. But men who marry women of a more suitable age and women who choose non-violent husbands are equally a product of their childhood; it is just a different childhood they are a product of.

In the psycho-analytic account, we begin life as savage infants, all animal instinct and need. We demand instant nipple, perfect feed, constant warmth, dry nappies, immediate comfort and a whole lot more besides; and we get angry when we do not get what we want. But the material world is indifferent to our demands. In a dog-eat-dog world, other people are more interested in getting their own needs satisfied than in satisfying babies' needs. Babies do not get just what they want, which is why they cry, get angry, or go passive to hide their anger and distress. Though we grow up physically, psychologically we remain demanding and unsatisfied infants. Whatever we seem to be on the surface as adults, underneath we are infantile male chauvinists, cavemen wielding a club in one hand and dragging a woman along by her hair in the other. Or we are

Little Red Riding Hoods, with the wolf not out in the forest but inside. We are certainly not, in Freud's account, the free and caring creatures we had once thought ourselves to be. Any sweet reasonableness we may have is only skin-deep and is achieved at a price. Society may tame us on the surface but the price we pay is frustration, anger, unsatisfied sex, neurosis.

And the civilized veneer is thin – the daily papers reveal just how thin when the veneer cracks and what is underneath crawls out. Sadism, sexual perversion, violence, incest, mugging, rape, murder, adultery like Herr Schmidt's . . . If we are inclined to dismiss all this as the activity of sick deviants, we should recollect the hunger and thirst of babies, their fury and violence when their demands are not met, their sexuality, the way they urinate and defecate without regard to time, place or the feelings of others. We should remember the savage infant that we all are, and the tyranny of our bodies.

As this – in Freud's view – is the way we are, he needs to explain how we get tamed and are turned into house-trained adults, even if the training goes only skin-deep. It happens in infancy, and what happens not only fits us for society but decides the kind of adult we become. The child is father to the adult in more ways than one. Freud believes that those early years not only make us human but also determine our different personalities and sort the men from the women. He explains the way this happens in his account of how personality develops.

Baby starts as just a bundle of instinct, needing to breathe, drink, urinate, eat, keep warm, be cuddled and stroked. Different parts of baby's body give sensual (even sexual) pleasure. The excitement of instinct, the pleasure of satisfaction, the pain of frustration, drive the body to action. 'Two sovereign masters, pain and pleasure,' says Bentham, 'govern us in all we do.'

At the start baby gets most pleasure from mouth, lips and tongue – Freud calls this the oral stage. In an ideal world it would be only pleasure that baby gets, but the real world being what it is and real mothers being fallible, baby also gets pain and anxiety from the oral area. Bits of energy and desire get stuck at this stage . . . and years later some of us are sucking away at sweets or cigarettes or sexual objects. The usual reason for getting fixated at this or any stage is too much or too little satisfaction – mothers can't win! Baby may be breast-fed for too long or enjoy the breast too much or have been kept on soft foods too long, and now is reluctant to move on to harder (and higher) things. Or baby may have been weaned too early or too rapidly or been frustrated because mother had difficulty with breast-feeding. The baby who is stuck or fixated at the early, sucking phase of the oral stage ends as a gullible adult, a sucker who swallows anything, is passive, helpless, dependent, over-fond of sipping drinks and of sweets, smoking, kissing. The baby stuck at the later, biting phase when teeth arrive ends up an oral sadistic personality. This is the sarcastic, assertive cynic whose comments have a cutting edge and whose very affection has bite.

From the age of nine months or so until the age of four, anus and bowels become a source of intense pleasure – and of pain and anxiety. Freud calls this the anal stage. Infants first enjoy the letting go, exploding out and expelling of faeces. Infants who get fixated at this early anal stage end up as men and women who surround themselves with mess in their homes and workplace, are always exploding emotionally and giving everyone a piece of their mind. These anal expulsive personalities are bossy, extravagant, ready to come right out with it and let you know how they feel. But these early pleasures and pains of letting faeces go or exploding out are soon replaced by those of bowel control as parents begin potty-training. Now the satisfaction and frustration of bowel control, of holding it in, of controlling events, become all-important. Whether energy and desire get stuck at this stage partly depends on how potty-training is handled: how early it is started and completed, how strictly the training regime is implemented, whether physical punishment, guilt, shame or praise are used. Infants fixated at this second stage end up very differently, as anal retentive personalities characterized by the late anal trio of tidiness, meanness and obstinacy. They are fastidious, obsessive, tidy adults who like everything in its place. They are careful individuals who hold on to things – money, stamps, old newspapers. They are stubborn people who refuse to change their habits or their minds.

The next stage is the one where Herr Schmidt got stuck, and Greek tragedy had hinted at its existence. Oedipus, having unknowingly killed his father, marries and sleeps with his mother. The gods punish him, of course! For Freud, the Oedipus myth is not the story of one unfortunate family but the eternal triangle at the heart of all families. It is not just a problem for Herr Schmidt and Oedipus, but for everyone. Oedipus' mistake lay in his turning into reality what for every other young male is just phantasy, and that is why the gods punished him.

At the age of four or five, children are incapable of reproduction. The boy's penis and the girl's clitoris are not adult sex organs, but they are nevertheless a source of great pleasure — and of anxiety and pain. When energy and desire get stuck at this stage they form what Freud calls the phallic personality. What makes them get stuck is not clear. Is it general excitement in the sex organs, or masturbation and how parents react? Whatever it is, according to Freud the adult personality that results is impulsive, self-centred, conforming. If male, a Casanova emerges, a 'great lover' full of himself; if female, a 'glamour girl'. Both are aware of their own attractiveness.

But, according to Freud, what makes the oedipus stage so important is not the phallic personality that may emerge but two other developments. First, the differences between the sexes begin here: at this stage boys become masculine and men, and girls become feminine and women. Secondly, in the process both acquire the conscience that characterizes human beings.

The sexual love of a man and a woman is exclusive, and the child that arrives as a result is an intruder. But the woman has to care for the child, and soon they have an 'affair' of their own going. If the child is a boy he comes to hate his father, since Father is a competitor for Mother. Freud's idea was not original. A century earlier, Diderot had observed: 'If left to ourselves and if our bodily strength came up to that of our phantasy, we would wring our fathers' necks and sleep with our mothers.' But the boy fears Father as well as hates him, and his terror becomes specific. He fears that this powerful and jealous man will castrate him. So he represses his sexual feelings for Mother and, acting on the principle that 'If you can't beat them, join them', comes to terms with his hatred and fear of Father by identifying with him. In this way, at least he possesses Mother vicariously. The boy's identification solves the oedipus conflict, and makes a man of him. By taking in Father's values along with Father, the boy acquires a conscience, which Freud calls the super-ego. The oedipus conflict will be familiar to anyone who has read *Sons and Lovers*, which was written by D. H. Lawrence before he had read Freud. The situation of Paul Morel, the hero of the novel, is made more difficult by his having a weak father whom the mother despises. This makes it harder for Paul to come through the oedipus stage in the usual way, by identifying with his father.

If the child is a girl, what happens is different since she is aware that she lacks a penis, or at least that her clitoris is smaller than a boy's penis. Freud says that the girl envies the male his 'superior' penis, and she comes to the conclusion that she must have been castrated. She blames her mother who (she knows or suspects) also suffers from having no penis, and this weakens her love for Mother. So she turns to Father who has the genuine article, loves him, and ends up happily wanting babies as a substitute for the much-envied male organ. It is often asserted that most mothers, as a hangover of penis envy, want sons rather than daughters. The girl now identifies with Mother, which makes a woman of her. She too acquires this unconscious conscience, the super-ego, by internalizing Mother's values.

With this solution to the oedipus conflict – or, as in the case of Herr Schmidt, the failure to find a solution – personality development is now over, according to Freud. No manipulative society – capitalist, partriarchal or whatever – has given us the personalities we have and have turned us into tough men who don't cry or into emotional women who do. Our personalities are the consequence of biology and family life; and family life is as inevitable as biology, since it takes two to make a baby. 'All women become like their mothers,' says Oscar Wilde. 'That is their tragedy. No man does. That's his.'

This second outcome of the oedipus stage, the unconscious

conscience called the super-ego, means that the savage infant is domesticated. When the child solves the oedipus conflict by identifying with Mother or Father and internalizing their values, the savage infant is turned into a 'civilized' adult. The adult who results may be scarred for life by the conflicts of those early years, but at least society can sleep peacefully in its bed, biology and parents having done their job. Though the child is still only five or six years old, in Freud's view nothing more of any psychological significance is going to happen.

In the latency stage that follows the oedipus conflict, those sexual instincts that were so important go underground. Children running noisily around in a primary school playground may be animals, but they are not sexual animals. Instinct and desire are marking time and nothing of any importance is happening.

When puberty arrives, the genital area becomes the chief source of pleasure again, with the body now capable of adult sex and reproduction. Energy and desire are at the genital stage – if after such an arduous and demanding journey any energy and desire are left! Much will be left behind, stuck in the oral, anal and oedipal phases. But if enough has got through, the result is Freud's genital personality, as much concerned with the needs and pleasures of others as with his or her own. This is obvious in the area of sex: any dog or chimp can copulate, but only the genital personality can have a relationship which the word 'love' implies.

In the beginning, in the gospel according to Freud, is the savage infant . . . is id, everything that is inherited and, above all, instinct. Instinct, the source of all energy and desire, is an innate pattern of behaviour like a bird's nest-building. Nest-building is triggered off by the bird's bodily mechanisms when the temperature rises in spring. Just as this instinct has its source in the bird's body so – for Freud – human instincts are located in the human body. Human instincts begin in the body but end in the mind. Hunger is a bodily need, but when I am hungry I *think* of cooking myself a meal, and hungry people *dream* of food. Thinking and dreaming happen in the mind. The puzzle of how body affects mind – the body–mind problem

21

– Freud side-steps by describing instincts as something in the mind. Though hunger and thirst and sex start in the body, what Freud takes as instinct is the lamb-chop which I think of cooking or the dreamed-of drink or the phantasied sex-object. In the beginning is body, instinct, the id, nothing else. As the child develops, mind emerges from body. But body remains all that there is and there is never anything more, according to Freud.

Originally Freud thought that there were two instincts and that both were a drive towards life. The ego instinct was about eating, drinking, defecating, about self-preservation generally, and the sexual instinct was about sex and about physical love, like affection for friends and children. But appalled by the carnage of the First World War Freud later proposed a death instinct.

Just before a party, or at any time of excitement, we thrill with tension. This is the life instinct (or Eros). In Freud's later, post-First World War view, the life instinct embraces the earlier ego and sexual instincts. The life instinct wants excitement and pleasure, it is the thrust of self-preservation, of uninhibited sex, of the move towards life. But there exists also a movement in the opposite direction. With the death instinct (or Thanatos), the body desires a return to the lifeless state in which it began. We enjoy the party and the stimulation of people and music and food and drink; but by the early hours we have had enough: we long to get away, to escape from the tension and excitement which are painful and too much for us now, and to sleep. 'The aim of all life,' said Freud in *Beyond the Pleasure Principle*, 'is death.' As we age, the tension of life's party becomes less pleasurable, perhaps even painful, and the desire to be rid of it grows; this is the death instinct. Turned in on ourselves, the death instinct causes masochism, self-destruction, suicide; directed outwards, it causes violence, aggression, war. The existence of a death instinct means that human aggression and violence are innate and explains the carnage of world wars by what is inherent in personality. Briefly, Freud changed his account from one in which instincts were about life and sex to one where they were about pleasure and aggression.

In his instinct theory Freud makes human beings seem rather like the plumbing. Instincts – our hunger and thirst, our need for sex, to defecate, and the rest – cause energy and desire to move through the mind like water moving through pipes under pressure. This energy and desire (which Freud calls libido) cause tension as they flow, looking for a breast to suck or a body to have intercourse with. When instincts are satisfied and the tension eliminated or reduced, we feel pleasure. When instincts are not satisfied, the tension becomes painful. Turn on the tap – eat, defecate, copulate, express your violence – and the water shoots out and the pressure is reduced. But what happens if we cannot turn on the tap and there is no way of regulating the pressure? Water does not contract, so pressure builds up. Something has got to give – and it could be the plumbing.

When energy and desire move around seeking discharge, there are only two possible outcomes, depending on whether the tap is on or off. If the tap is on, water shoots out. Baby is fed or defecates; the adult drinks, eats, has intercourse. Mental energy and desire find pleasurable release, and our instincts are satisfied. If the tap is not on, the pressure of blocked instinct builds up and tension increases. Baby is not breast-fed; the toddler is not allowed to defecate here and now; the adult has nothing to eat or to drink, or no one to have intercourse with. Such frustration is painful.

In the plumbing situation – if the plumbing is any good – pressure cannot increase to dangerous levels because of built-in controls. But human beings have no built-in controls, so something has to happen. One alternative is that no way out is found by frustrated instinct and pressure builds up till a pipe bursts at some weak point, and water pours out. The weak points will be those where energy and desire got stuck in childhood at the oral, anal and phallic stages; water pouring out is someone having a mental breakdown. The other alternative is that frustrated instinct checks back on itself, like water at a blocked outlet, and is forced to find a way out through an overflow pipe. These overflow pipes which frustrated instinct escapes by are called defence mechanisms.

Leonardo da Vinci was the child of an unmarried peasant woman. She cared for him until he was four, when his father took him away to be brought up by a new wife. In an essay on Leonardo, Freud declares that in those early years an erotic relationship grew up between the boy and his natural mother. The 'affair' was brought to a traumatic end when the boy was taken away by his father. A tap was turned off and energy and desire were blocked; the new mother did not manage to turn the tap back on. The boy was forced by the rupture to repress his sexual feelings for his natural mother. As an adult, Leonardo was detached, aloof, something of a loner, and not very sexual. On one occasion, according to Freud, his defences slipped and repressed erotic feelings for his mother broke through: this was when he painted the *Mona Lisa* and is the secret of her smile. Leonardo has returned to childhood, to the mother he was physically wrenched from but whom he never left emotionally. The smile is his mother's and expresses an erotic tenderness that seduced the boy and bound him to her for ever. 'Gotcha,' it says. Leonardo, usually quite careless about his paintings, was obsessed with the *Mona Lisa*. There was no tap he could turn on to release his desire for his mother, so pressure had been reduced by siphoning it off through an overflow pipe. That overflow pipe was the defence mechanism of sublimation, the sublimation of painting. After all, what is art (in Freud's view) but an escape from the pain of frustrated instincts? There may have been pain and longing still – hence the haunting smile – but at least unbearable breakdown was avoided.

Sublimation, for Freud, is the aristocrat of defence mechanisms. If human beings are such creatures of biology and instinct, how do art, language, music, science, thought, technology, care and concern for others originate? They originate through sublimation, Freud answers. In sublimation, what instinct really wants, to enjoy Mother's breasts or to attack Father, is replaced by 'higher' goals; and frustrated energy and desire are redirected to these other goals. My hostility for Father is diverted into my work as a surgeon or a butcher. Just watch me with a scalpel or a cleaver! Sublimation is a superior defence mechanism, healthy, free from anxiety, not neurotic.

In Freud's account the jammed-up quality of all defence mechanisms, their tendency to become self-perpetuating, is turned by sublimation into something positive: independence. Art, science, human relationships and culture originate in our frustrated instincts; but once set in motion by sublimation they continue, independent of their humble origins. Freud sees all civilization originating in the human capacity to sublimate frustrated instinct. Unfortunately we do not always quite manage it, and the result is breakdown. In *Civilization and its Discontents* Freud writes, 'Neurosis is the price we pay for civilization.'

Freudian sublimation is an impressive idea but it leaves a question mark. Are such achievements as the *Mona Lisa*, Bach's *St Matthew Passion*, relativity theory, or putting men on the Moon the result of *nothing but* frustrated instinct? Common sense senses that there is more to it than that; and at this point one begins to be concerned about the adequacy of Freud's reductionist 'nothing-but' explanations. Leonardo's childhood may have been a factor in the making of the *Mona Lisa*, but is his painting 'nothing but' the product of a deprived childhood? Other artists with similar deprived childhoods could paint something on similar lines which would not move us at all. What makes the *Mona Lisa* a great painting, one which touches us deeply, is not explained by Leonardo's longing for his mother.

Freud lists other defence mechanisms, but none as healthy as sublimation. Repression is the one all others depend on, including sublimation. In repression, unacceptable ideas and impulses are pushed down, to fester in the unconscious. But the feelings attached to these impulses and ideas remain active. As a baby, Casanova was never loved and caressed, and consequently feels unloved and worthless as an adult. He represses the painful memories of those uncherished years, but they live on, active though unconscious. All other Freudian defence mechanisms begin with the unconscious activity of repression.

In denial we refuse to accept an unpleasant truth and we repress it. This may be a temporary, unacceptable experience like a mother's denial that her teenage daughter's jeering has made her furious. It may be a refusal to accept a more permanent truth, such as my being full of envy – though this may be obvious to everyone except myself. In the defence mechanism of projection, what is mine – my sadness, my sexual desires, my anger – is repressed and pushed on to someone else. 'I'm not depressed. I'm fine. It's my wife who's depressed' ... 'It's disgusting the way young people are so obsessed with sex these days' ... 'I'm not hostile. They are' ... or even, 'I'm not hostile. They are and they are persecuting me.'

In Freudian reaction formation, unacceptable ideas are coped with by parading the opposite. In his dream Herr Schmidt masks his hostile feelings for his dying friend (or father) by kissing and embracing him. Casanova hides from himself his feeling of being worthless and unloved by acting aggressively and promiscuously. But however effective this siphoning off, the feeling remains; and Casanova, for all his aggression and sexual prowess, feels powerless and unloved still. The underlying experience does not cease to exist just because it has been repressed into the unconscious.

In the defence mechanism of rationalization, we put out a good (but false) story to hide the truth about our motives. A woman beats her child severely, and the reality is that she lost her temper and enjoyed hitting him. This is unacceptable, so she hides the truth from herself and from others, by maintaining that she punished the child for his own good and that it hurt her more than it hurt him. Rationalization moves to the offensive by hiding the real, sordid motive behind an impressive one. This makes rationalization dangerous – as the graffiti said, 'There is no fury like that of a vested interest masquerading as a moral principle.'

In everyday life we usually have to make do with second best, and babies quickly learn this sad truth. But if what we really want eventually comes along, we usually grab it. Given the chance, we suck the breast, kick our younger brother, copulate. But, according to Freud, defence mechanisms are not content to make do only until the real thing arrives. By the time the real thing does arrive we may have built so big a barrier, possibly with our anger, that we cannot now accept it, and so we stick to our substitute. As a baby, a woman longed to be touched and stroked, but never was; now, as an adult, she cannot bear anything so intimate as a caress and goes her own solitary way. Defence mechanisms become self-perpetuating and independent of their origins, making do with second-best substitutes for ever.

The image shifts from plumbing to something more dignified. Freud's men and women, emerging in the wake of nineteenth-century Romanticism, are tragic heroes worthy of Shelley and Byron. They stand on a mountain, the music of Beethoven or Mahler playing in the background, shaking their fists, Nietzsche-like, at the heavens. Life and the universe never fulfil their desires and hopes and never will, and they know it. They experience an abyss between what they want and what they get. Freud explains this experience in two laws governing human behaviour, the pleasure principle and the reality principle.

Watch any baby – in the psycho-analytic account it wants only one thing: to have its needs satisfied. Whether baby or adult, we all operate on a pleasure-pain calculus: to get the greatest pleasure from having our instincts satisfied, and to avoid the pain of frustration. This is Freud's pleasure principle. According to Freud, all 'higher' activities like thinking and remembering come into existence only to get instincts satisfied, and are secondary. Hungry people in concentration camps think of food, not art and ideas. In prisons where the food is adequate the inmates are not concerned with good books, fashion and bingo, but are obsessed by sex.

The reality principle is ... Unfortunately the world is not accommodating. Breasts are not always available for baby, certainly not instantly, and when they arrive, they usually fail to provide the exact suck and flow of milk that baby wants. The same goes for the rest of life. Reality does not put in our path the means of gratifying our instincts as and when we require. A young male may desire the latest sex symbol but he will have to make do with the girl next door, and only in her own good time. My thirst, my hunger, my need to be held, to defecate, to have sexual intercourse, are not satisfied by the real world to my specifications. One may long for a lager but have to make do with water until the pubs open; in other areas of the world, many have to wait for just a cup of water. In childhood, frustration of instincts is more traumatic than in adult life because babies have no sense of the future. Thirsty, wet and uncomfortable, babies cannot reassure themselves that a breastful of milk or a dry warm nappy is on the way. Whatever we really want, as babies we learn to take what is going. It is the best we can get; it is all we can get. The attempt to get satisfaction from what the real world has to offer is the Freudian reality principle.

So, according to the psycho-analytic account, the individual develops a monitoring process to reality-test the external world. This is the ego. The ego monitors in order to discover what exists in the real world to satisfy instinct, and how to get it. The material world may have to be worked on and modified, perhaps by moving a chair to climb on a table. Technology begins here. It may be necessary to cry, coo, smile, throw a tantrum, sulk or whatever. What the ego's reconnaissance inevitably discovers is that the demands of our instincts will have to be modified, deferred, scaled down. You may feel furious and want to smash a colleague in the face, but you will have to make do with taking your rage out on the squash court.

The reality principle is no killjoy saying 'Can't'. But humans soon learn that the only way to get real and not phantasy satisfactions is by accommodating to the world. The ego is a realist. Operating according to the reality principle, the ego sorts out what pleasures are possible and how to get them, and what pains can be avoided. But the pleasures of the real world are paltry. In the Freudian (and Romantic) view, humans imagine for themselves more in the way of pleasure and satisfaction than they can possibly obtain. Humans have to scale down their desire and aspirations (and erections) to the pathetic and minuscule satisfactions that the world and human biology can offer. We want so much and get so little; that is the tragedy of life – though with a touch it becomes farce. 'Pass me my teeth,' says the old man in bed with the beautiful young woman, 'I want to bite you.' But beneath the humour there is sadness, the sadness of Freud's stoic pessimism.

So the ego monitor comes into existence because instincts are frustrated – wet and uncomfortable nappies are not changed and breasts are not available immediately. Freud's emphasis is always on body. If there were no bodily frustration, there would be no mind or ego. Indeed, in Freud's view, if there were no frustration there would be no personality. Ego, mind, personality emerge only to serve the needs of id. If the body could get its needs satisfied without any ego to reconnoitre and to monitor, no thinking, remembering, imagining mind would develop. Body, id, instinct come first, and mind and ego develop merely to make sure that these get what they want. But the result is that, where once there was only body, mind now exists. Freud is saying that mind and ego develop in order to get instincts satisfied; they come about because they are useful. But how actually this development of ego and mind happens Freud does not explain, nor does he explain what mind is.

A woman looks out of the window, wondering if the good weather will last, and she remembers last year's summer holiday. This is conscious mind at work – she is aware of what she is thinking and remembering. But Freud believed that conscious mind is only the tip of the iceberg, the small bit of mind above water. While on holiday the woman saw a dog drown, but she has no recollection of this and does not even remember when her husband mentions the unpleasant incident. The memory is repressed. Repressed memories and thoughts are not conscious and cannot be brought to mind – or only with difficulty. But some time ago, walking by a river, she suddenly felt anxious and depressed and did not know why. The memory of the dog drowning, though repressed, is active and still affects her. This is the Freudian unconscious at work, repressed but active. Soon, without realizing it, the woman begins to avoid rivers.

Post-hypnotic suggestion illustrates – and is evidence for – an unconscious. 'In a moment I will wake you and you will return to your seat,' says the hypnotist, 'and in five minutes you will stand up and sing the National Anthem.' Five minutes later, the man stands up and – to his own astonishment and embarrassment – sings *God Save the Queen*. In Freud's account of the unconscious, unacceptable thoughts and memories and desires are pushed from conscious mind and are kept out. They remain unconscious because they are actively repressed, and any attempt by them to surface into conscious mind is resisted. But the feelings attached to them escape. The woman cannot remember the dog drowning but anxiously avoids rivers. Herr Schmidt, because of an unconscious oedipus conflict, excitedly pursues married women. Leonardo, his sexual feelings for his mother repressed, paints the *Mona Lisa* with a smile of mocking eroticism on her face.

In the beginning is id, the instinctual infant that each of us is at birth, a little monster that greedily seeks pleasure, demands satisfaction, and gets angry when its demands are not met. Like Moby Dick, the white whale, for the most part id is beneath the surface, its presence apparent only from the flotsam of destruction it leaves in its wake. The id is unconscious.

The ego develops on the 'surface of the id', monitoring the real world to satisfy the demands of the infant. Phantasies are all very well, but in the end one prefers the real thing. A real if imperfect nipple to suckle is better than a perfect phantasy one. A real cuddle from the girl or boy next door is more satisfying than a dream embrace from the latest sex symbol. The ego is the organization of our conscious mind and it thinks, remembers, imagines. The ego is the executive of personality, and if id is the horse which supplies energy and desire, then ego is the rider that controls . . . but not entirely. To remain in the saddle, ego sometimes has to go where id takes it. Id remains the main part of personality, the eight-ninths of the iceberg beneath the water. When id's demands cannot be satisfied, ego resorts to defence mechanisms such as projection, reaction formation and – best of all – sublimation.

The final element in Freud's threefold structure of personality is super-ego, the internalized parent of the same sex. It is the unconscious conscience which results from the resolution of the oedipus conflict. What does super-ego do? It does what any anxious parent would: it orders the ego about, judges it, threatens it with punishment. But super-ego is nothing like traditional conscience (or parent), nothing so gentle as that. After all, the anger it contains is nobody else's but my own. It is my hostility for my father, my would-be castrator, turned back on myself. It is the daughter's hostility for her mother, whom the girl blames for her lack of penis, turned against herself. In the beginning is the savage infant and an explosive confrontation between biology and society. By the end of childhood, society is victorious, the infant ejected from the paradise of pure instinct, and ego and super-ego are in control, but only just. In Freud's view, beneath the civilized veneer the law of the jungle survives. The id lives on, a savage infant in adult clothing.

There are many criticisms of Freud. His emphasis on the unchanging biology of human beings – anatomy is destiny – is called in question by other theorists. As we shall see, both Skinner and the social behaviourists do not regard our unchanging biology as all-important, since human behaviour is malleable and easily altered by the environment. Anthropologists too see personality as shaped and changed by the circumstances of different cultures. After all, the same human biology is found everywhere, but different societies – France and India, Italy and China, the north and south of England – produce different personalities and behaviour. Common-sense observation in a multicultural society confirms that people from different cultures are different. Perhaps personality is not as determined by biology and as unchanging as Freud thinks.

Nor is the individual so much a product of history and so totally stuck in the past as Freud says he is. Freud made us aware of the importance of our first five or six years, but common sense tells us he got it only partly right. Yes, what happens in childhood stays with us – and we should be grateful to Freud for adding this understanding to common sense. But common sense is aware that people can and do change, though with difficulty. Other theories suggest (and common observation confirms) that people like Herr Schmidt will not inevitably be pursuing married women for the rest of their lives.

Women come off badly in Freud. He seems to have believed that men are superior and that women envy them, and women not only feel inferior but they are – castrated in both body and mind. The most that can be said in his defence is that Freud may have captured an historical truth. If everything in a culture combines to impress on women that they are inferior to men, eventually they may come to believe it. This was probably the situation in Freud's Europe. If women envied the penis in the Vienna of his day, it was because men had a better time. What they envied was not the male organ, or being male, but only what it represented: having a better time because you are a man. But this means that Freud's account is not a universal account of personality, just good reporting of the 'facts' and feelings of his own day.

A recent accusation is that Freud's theory of the oedipus complex is not even good reporting but was based on a distortion of the 'facts'. The accusation is that the women who came to see Freud really had been sexually molested as children, and that Freud knew this. Realizing that he would arouse great hostility by saying children were often seduced, Freud chose to regard the sexual abuse his patients remembered as mere phantasy. He then took these 'phantasy' seductions as evidence of the women's own sexuality as children, and as the basis for his oedipus theory.

Whatever the truth of this accusation, certainly the fact that most of Freud's patients were middle-class Viennese women, may have made his theory provincial and specific to one social class. Moreover, the structure of the family varies from culture to culture more than Freud realized. Perhaps the oedipus conflict occurs only where the family is close-knit and nuclear and where the male is dominant. And many theorists since Freud, including the neo-Freudians, have stressed the influence on personality of the wider society beyond and outside the family.

Are there really no significant changes in personality after the age of five, or six if you are a late developer? Does nothing of any importance occur in the latency stage? Erikson, a neo-Freudian, and most primary school teachers would disagree. They point out that children at this stage acquire (or fail to acquire) competence and confidence in bodily and social skills, and in mental skills like intelligence, language, memory. Instinctual activity may be quiet and latent at this stage, but what Freud fails to see is that much else besides instinct is important for human beings. His account, here as elsewhere, is partial.

Does nothing of any importance occur during puberty? Are there no crises of identity and beliefs to be sorted out by teenagers? And when the mature personality arrives, how has this genital adult suddenly become capable of concern for others and love? Freud does not even make clear what 'love' is. With the arrival of adulthood and the genital personality, is there no more development at all? None, says Freud. Freud believed that after the oedipus stage, when the structure of personality is established, human life is largely repetition. The bodily changes of puberty and beyond are not accompanied by psychological changes. But while no one now doubts the importance of those first few years, common sense knows that what happens after five or six is not like the re-run of an old movie, and adult life is not just a repeat of childhood on a broader stage. Our experience suggests – and psychologists like Carl Rogers emphasize – a capacity for change and growth possessed by adults.

Freud's account of humans as bundles of instincts, and a bit like the plumbing, raises problems. We shall see that it is difficult to discover the person that each of us is in such a system of instincts. But the idea of instincts raises a more general criticism of much of Freudian theory, and the death instinct illustrates this. How would you decide whether a death instinct exists? We all die in the end – but this is hardly proof! Large areas of psycho-analytic theory resemble the death instinct in not being scientifically testable. How do you test the idea of repression, since repression is an unconscious activity? 'I am not aware of repressing sexual feelings for my mother,' says the patient. 'Of course not,' says the analyst, 'your repression is unconscious.' Heads I win, tails you lose! Where it is possible to test scientifically, the results are mixed. For example, there is no evidence for a phallic personality, slight evidence for an oral personality, and rather more for the anal, especially the late anal, personality.

In Freud's view, there is nothing moral about human beings, in spite of the super-ego. It is pleasure we seek, pleasure and nothing else, even when it comes to people. What we want from others in sex is not intimacy or love or a relationship, but pleasure. If this seems like treating someone as a 'sex object', then this is what they are. Freud seems to take as normal human behaviour what common sense regards as debased. In

Freud's view, others exist as means to our own ends – no wonder he thinks so little of people! Significantly, neo-Freudians such as Fromm reject Freud's pleasure-obsessed account in order to assert what most of us already know: that people need people, and not just for what they can get out of them. In the practice of Freudian psycho-analysis, there is usually no problem. Analysts working in therapy ignore such theoretical nonsense as instinctual gratification being all that really matters, and stick to Freud's therapeutic insights and their own common-sense knowledge of others.

In Freud's view there is no genuinely moral dimension in human beings. But if we all struggled with no holds barred to grab what pleasure we could, our situation would be no different from that of other animals in the jungle of evolution, where only the fittest survive. Freud sees humans as substituting in its place a human jungle, the *laissez-faire* market of exchange, bargaining and power relationships. We really want unlimited food, sex, revenge – but so does everyone else. If we give up some demands and scale down the rest, others will do the same. This is what society offers: limit your demands and others will limit theirs. It ensures that we are less at risk from the greed, sexuality and violence of others, and they are safe from ours. In the end, we all benefit. Some freedom has to be sacrificed, but much of this so-called freedom is only the licence of the jungle. We accept society's offer; we have no alternative.

Freud's account of morality is nothing like the mutual-reinforcement society of behaviourism. But then the parties to the contract that psycho-analysis describes are not the plasticine people of behaviourism but infants with hard biologies and greedy instincts. There is nothing moral about the super-ego. What stops each of us exploiting, assaulting and raping others is that it would lead to others doing the same to us, and the lawlessness of the jungle would prevail. Morality is enlightened self-interest. Right and wrong, good and bad, are not laws written in the human heart by God or evolution. They are only market-place rules, agreed for our own safety. What appears to be right or wrong is only what society allows or forbids. Though at times society's laws and orders are harsh, we should be grateful for the protection that they afford us from each other. So we agree this social contract since it seems to be in our interest to do so. But any supposed morality is simply this contract internalized in the unconscious super-ego. We know we could get away with anti-social behaviour occasionally, but if we did, others would do the same and society would collapse ... But why – if Freud's view of personality is correct – should anyone be concerned about society collapsing? Why – it is reasonable to ask – should anyone be *concerned* about anything if there is no real moral element in our personality?

When a mother told Freud she intended to bring up her children according to psycho-analytic principles, he told her: 'Do as you please, it's sure to turn out badly.' Freud had no high opinion of human beings, though words with a moral flavour like 'good', 'bad', 'evil' are meaningless in psycho-analysis. Wanting to murder Father and go to bed with Mother is no more wrong than a dolphin wanting its next meal of fish. But acting out such phantasies is dangerous. We would not describe an Alsatian which savaged a child as evil, but we would have the dog destroyed.

Human beings are too dangerous to be let loose on the streets without strict controls, which is why society has to be repressive. Look at what happens when schoolboys – and English public-school ones at that – find themselves on a desert island without any restraining authority. In a short time they are murdering each other; and it is because we recognize the adult world and ourselves in William Golding's *Lord of the Flies* that we find the novel so powerful. After all, the book ends with the boys returning to a world war in which adults are killing one another on a much vaster scale, with no one to intervene and stop them. Other scientific accounts of personality, such as Carl Rogers', see human beings as essentially good. But if Freud's humans were in the zoo, 'These animals are dangerous' would be written above the cage.

In its estimation of people, the Freudian account resembles the Christian doctrine of Original Sin. But though Freud regards human beings as dangerous, he would not describe them as sinful or bad, since this implies choice. Freud believed that humans have little or no choice. After all, why does Hamlet dither so about avenging his father's death? Hamlet had a normal childhood, and at four or five, like any healthy lad, he desired his mother and wanted to be rid of his father. Hamlet partly solved his oedipus conflict in the usual way, by repression and identifying with his father. Identification is characterized by idealizing, and Hamlet does rather put the late king on a pedestal.

Matters were made difficult for Hamlet by having a mother who doted on him at the oedipal stage, since this formed a strong erotic bond between them. Imagine, then, how Hamlet felt when his uncle did what, deep down and long ago, he had wanted to do: kill Father and jump into bed with Mother! All that repressed desire and hostility were aroused in the unconscious, and enough of the old conflict returned to make him dither. His erotic feelings for his mother were re-awakened, as the sexual overtones of the bedroom scene make clear. His entreaty to her to withdraw from his uncle's bed is hardly appropriate coming from a son to his mother! The scene ends with Hamlet killing Polonius in a fit of rage, mistaking him for the uncle, his new stepfather, who is now the rival for Mother's affections. But when Hamlet has time to reflect, he cannot bring himself to kill his uncle. How can he kill the man who has done what he always wanted to do: murder Father and sleep with Mother? Uncle is almost an *alter ego*. No wonder Hamlet dithers – or seems to!

Hamlet only seems to dither because – in spite of 'To be, or not to be' – he really has no choice. Hamlet is not free to choose since what he does is caused and already decided for him. In Freud's view all human behaviour is caused and inevitable, and no one is free to choose. Freud is a hard determinist, and in *A Short Account of Psycho-Analysis* he regarded as central to psycho-analysis 'the thorough-going meaningfulness and determinism of even the apparently most obscure and arbitrary mental phenomena'. What is more obscure than a dream or more arbitrary than a slip of the tongue? But our night-life of dreams, and our daytime slips of the tongue and lapses of memory, all mean something. They mean something because they are not arbitrary but caused. What all of us do, including

Hamlet, is largely caused by the id's unconscious desires, thoughts, conflicts.

A man can remember only the maiden name of a woman he has always desired. He represses her married name because he wants to think of her as still unmarried and sexually available. 'Push off,' says a woman to a 'friend' on the other side of a jammed door, intending to say, 'Push.' Freud regards such lapses of memory, slips of the tongue and the content of dreams as caused by the unconscious. He believes that both the workings of mind and our behaviour are caused. Human life is governed by our bodies and past experience, and there is no freedom in our supposed choices.

In *Parapraxes* Freud makes his position clear: 'You nourish the illusion of there being such a thing as psychical freedom, and you will not give it up. I am sorry to say I disagree with you categorically over this.' The illusion that we are free persists because the causes of our thoughts, supposed choices and actions are unconscious and we are unaware of them. But the causes are there none the less, in the innate instincts of the id and in our past experience, particularly at the oral, anal and oedipal stages of childhood. Other accounts of personality which regard human behaviour as caused place the causes in present circumstances. Some accounts regard humans as free ... and even Freud is not completely certain about his hard determinism.

The plots of several of Jane Austen's novels turn on a young woman who first flirts with a man of her own age but who ends by marrying an esteemed if dull father-figure. The young heroine has usually had a worthy father but a trivial mother, and in the novel there is not much to be said for sexual passion. What we have here is an unsolved oedipus conflict, in a woman called an electra complex – though the term did not originate with Freud and he was never happy with it. The heroine has not resolved her complex because she could not identify with the trivial mother, and so she marries this dull, dependable substitute for her father.

But in *Persuasion*, Jane Austen's last novel, things are different. The heroine's mother is dead, the father shallow and

trivial; she marries a man her own age whom she loves passion-
ately. Human behaviour, including the writing of a novel, is
largely caused, and Jane Austen's plots were dictated by her
inner unconscious world. By the time she came to write *Persuasion* something had changed, and she realized that she had
sacrificed her life for her sisters and a selfish father. What had
been unconscious, and determined what Jane wrote, became
conscious, and made freedom possible. Side by side with his
hard determinism, Freud also held that when human beings are
conscious they are capable of a modest degree of freedom.

In this second view, what is unconscious is caused and determined, and what is conscious can be free. If the man could
admit his sexual feelings for the married woman, he might
begin to remember her married name. What would be the point
of Freud sitting for hours in his consulting-room if he did not
believe that people could change? Psycho-analytic therapy is
possible only if what people think and do is not entirely caused
and if they can occasionally choose. Freud believed that humans
could be free when the mind is conscious. If the Prince of
Denmark had insight into his situation and realized he was in
the wrong play – it should have been *Oedipus Rex*, not *Hamlet* –
the plot might have developed differently. If Herr Schmidt
became conscious of his oedipus problem, it would stop his
being attracted to married women only. But Freud avoids an
obvious problem: how does what is unconscious and caused
become conscious and free? Is this change caused (and determined) or is it the result of a free choice by the individual?
There is no explanation.

But Freud believed that free choice was very limited, and he
made this clear in the modest aim he gave to therapy: to transform hysterical misery into everyday unhappiness. He believed
that most of the mind's activity is unconscious, and therefore
caused. But even such a modest (and unexplained) degree of
freedom is incompatible with hard determinism and is inconsist-
ent with Freud's dogmatic assertion of 'the thorough-going . . .
determinism of even the apparently most obscure and arbitrary
mental phenomena'.

What are these 'mental phenomena'? What is mind, whether

of the conscious or the unconscious variety? Radical behaviourists say that mind is illusion, but Freud never doubted
the reality of mind. Again, what would be the point of listening
to people talking about anxieties, phobias, depression, if mind
and thought were illusion? Mind makes people ill. Mind causes
paralysis in hysteria, trembling and sweating in anxiety, the
disturbed behaviour of psychosis. By working on mind, psycho-
analytic therapy can cure some of this.

But in what way mind is real is the old problem; as a materialist, Freud would like to have shown that mind was body and
brain. He could then have come up with explanations like: 'The
Mona Lisa has a teasing smile because of the high level of
testerone in Leonardo's body when he was painting.' Nowhere
does Freud explain the workings of Leonardo's mind or anyone
else's by direct reference to body. But he wanted to, and in his
early 'Project for a Scientific Psychology' he tried to produce an
explanation that would do just that: move directly from body
and brain to mind. Within a short time he described his Project
as balderdash, and he never published it. He was a biological
reductionist who believed that everything about human beings,
including mind, could be reduced to body.

Freud was pulled in two directions. First, mind was real and
could not (as yet) be explained by biology, so psycho-analytic
treatment had to work with mind. The language of common
sense with insight was used in therapy: 'You are depressed
because you envy your sister' . . . 'You are anxious because you
harbour an unconscious hatred of your father'. Freud was pulled
a second way, in the direction of that sort of scientific account
in which only the physical was real and where mind was part of
body. But it would be absurd to adopt such scientific talk in
therapy: 'You are depressed because your noradrenaline levels
are upset' . . . 'You feel anxious because your sympathetic nervous system is over-aroused'.

Freud believed that mind and the stuff of mind such as
thoughts, memories and phantasies were real, but he did not
know what they were. So in practice he resorted to the
common-sense dualist position that human beings have minds
and bodies and that these interact. He did not know how they

interacted, but he avoided the problem by giving an account of mind and personality in terms of mind and the psychological. At the same time he conveyed the dependence of mind and personality on body and biology by using terms like instinct, id, libido and unconscious. But Freud does not explain what mind is, nor how it interacts with body.

One might think that Freud has explained how mind comes about, but his account is inadequate. To say that mind and the ego 'emerge' from id because the id experiences frustration is no explanation. A proper explanation would give the steps by which this happens. It is scarcely adequate to assert that mind and the conscious ego come into being because they are useful!

And how can id experience the frustration by which mind and ego come about if there is not already something like an 'I' to experience frustration? According to common sense there exists an 'I' that feels tension, suffers pain, enjoys pleasure, defends against anxiety. According to Freud the ego emerges from the id to maximize our pleasure and minimize our pain. But what is it in each of us that experiences that pleasure and pain in the first place? Nowhere in Freud's account is there this 'I' that each of us has – or is – and which is on the receiving end of so much tension, pain, pleasure, anxiety. The ego cannot be the 'I', because the Freudian ego comes into existence to ensure our pleasure and protect us from pain. The 'I' must already feel pleasure and pain before this can happen. There can be no experience unless the 'I' or something equivalent already exists to have the experience.

As we shall see, in Mead's social behaviourism there is clearly an 'I' that experiences. In the practice of psycho-analytic therapy, the analyst adopts the ideas and language of common sense and assumes the existence of a person, of an 'I' desiring and wishing, loving and hating. But it is difficult to find such a person in Freud. In his account of personality there appears no one to whom we can say, 'You want, you know, you feel.' All that can be said is: the ego wants, knows, feels. What is missing is not immediately obvious because Freud is vague, and common sense fills the gaps. In his account of personality Freud presents the person as a meeting-place of forces. Instinct theory sees personality as a river-valley where waters collide with turbulence. What is thought, desired or felt is the outcome of opposing forces, like the path a river takes after its tributaries meet. Freud breaks down the human being into conscious and unconscious, ego, super-ego, id and instincts. Any theorist who fragments personality has to put Humpty-Dumpty together again to leave us with a person, an I, a real you or me. Freud does not do this.

Freud's ideas originated largely in his clinical work with patients. It has been objected that these were few in number and were mainly middle-class, middle-aged Viennese women. It is also pointed out that Freud made notes *after* therapy sessions when he might not have remembered everything. But it does not greatly matter how a theory originates – a hunch or a dream will do. In the end what matters is how useful it is, how correct it is, and – if it is to be scientific – how testable it is.

And Freud provides an astonishing wealth of knowledge, insight and an original perspective on human personality. With psycho-analytic therapy he instituted a new approach to the treatment of mental illness. He made us aware of how society, in the shape of parents, forms conscience and 'morality'. He revealed the influence of childhood experience on adult personality, and exposed the reality of sexual feelings in children. He focused our attention on the power of biology and instinct, and he pointed to an apparent absence of freedom in human life. What we think and do is largely the result of our bodily needs and our history: and this is true as much for the great achievements of culture, art and science as for our slips of the tongue, and what we laugh at and forget. With the perspective Freud provided, we realize that human beings are not as rational and reasonable as we once thought but are sexual, aggressive, unconscious. The human animal is dangerous – so dangerous that a stiff dose of law and order is needed, and society has to be repressive for it to become a safe place to live in.

When it comes to psycho-analytic therapy, what is striking is the common-sense nature of the explanations adopted. In therapy the talk is of 'wanting your mother's approval' . . . 'trying

to be like your mother so as to win your father's love' ...
'hating your sister because you felt your mother preferred her'.
This is supplemented by an extraordinary wealth of psychological insights, particularly with the idea of the unconscious.
When the boy weeps at the grave of Pushkin's dog it is his dead
mother, the psycho-analyst realizes, that the boy is crying
for. But common sense is supplemented, not supplanted, by a
psycho-analytic account. We are still talking about grief and the
pain of loss, not about tension reduction or ego defences or death
instincts. The psycho-analyst does not make interpretations
like 'Your id seeks tension reduction' but suggests, 'You wanted
her to die so you could have your mother all to yourself.'
The psycho-analyst does not comment, 'The ego is defending
against anxiety,' but says, 'Your son leaving home brought back
the feelings you had as a child when your sister died.' Freudian
ideas and insights add great depth to the analysis which common
sense provides, but they do not usually replace common sense.

Freud's emphasis on biology underplays the power of society
and culture to shape personality and behaviour. One has only to
read of other societies or observe them on television to realize
how different people are – though how deep that difference
goes is a matter for research. If Freud had been more aware of
the influence of society on behaviour, he need not have resorted
to the idea of a death instinct to explain human violence and
aggression. He might have regarded the collective violence of
the First World War as originating in society and culture rather
than in the instinctual nature of individuals. And perhaps there
is more to parent–child relationships than the feeding, toilet-
training, sexuality which Freud's preoccupation with instinct
emphasizes. Common observation and an informed and enlightened common sense would suggest that love and caring and
concern matter too.

But Freud's real failures are more radical. He did not solve
the problem of whether human beings are free. He recognizes
no moral element in human beings. Since he believes that
humans are largely not free he cannot hold that there is
any moral dimension, since one can be moral only if one is
free. In Freud's account the difference between a Stalin and a

Gandhi comes down to a difference in biology (which is ridiculous) or a difference in childhoods (which may be relevant but is not the whole explanation). If he explains the Hitlers and Stalins of this world, which is doubtful, he certainly does not account for the Gandhis and the Mother Teresas. If we believed Freud, we would empty all our prisons and turn them into mental hospitals. We do not do this because we suspect that there is a moral element in human beings, and that sometimes they are free and responsible for what they do. Finally, Freud fails to solve the problems of mind. The conscious 'I' that common sense recognizes disappears in Freud, leaving personality without a person.

Freud certainly provides a perspective on humans, but humans transcend Freud's account of them, which is partial and one-dimensional. There are – as we shall see – other dimensions to personality, and other perspectives.

Chapter Three

PIGEON PEOPLE:

B. F. Skinner's behaviourism

Our personality is the product of our conduct.

Aristotle: *Ethics*

In contrast to Freud's pessimism, Skinner claims we have yet to discover what man can make of man. In his novel *Walden Two*, he outlines the utopia his view of personality makes possible. It is a society without class, where all are equal. Everyone works four hours a day on average because, with organization and modern technology, nothing more is needed. No one is paid, but a credit scheme operates and credits are given for unpleasant jobs. If you wish to work only two hours a day, it will have to be in the sewers. If you want a more pleasant workplace like the flower garden, you will have to put in over the four hours. By manipulating credits in this way managers (whose work also is credit-rated) make all jobs equally desirable. In spite of so little time being spent working, there is no problem of leisure since music-making, acting, writing and all the arts and crafts flourish.

In *Walden Two* stable marriages are approved of, but when they fail no one is blamed. Who is to blame, and for what? There were just not the right conditions. Children suffer less when marriages fail because the whole community is responsible, not just the biological parents. In this scientific age children should be in the care of experts, not of untrained amateurs called mothers and fathers. With the whole community responsible, adults can enjoy all children, not just their own, and children can benefit from all adults. Envy and competitiveness are avoided.

Skinner's utopia has no need for the constraints of repression, law and order which Freud believed necessary. But *Walden*

Two is not the untested phantasy of a political dreamer because, according to Skinner, its foundations rest firmly on scientific behaviourist psychology. Behaviourist principles are used as a basis for making society as pleasant and painless as possible. Then, using the same principles, people are shaped as pleasantly and painlessly as possible to fit that society. Violence and jealousy, competitiveness and other destructive behaviour can be eliminated and human happiness made possible. All that is needed is the right conditions.

We begin by making society as pleasant as possible and shaping people to fit in, but even the best society has frustrations. Everyday life teaches us to tolerate frustration but we learn haphazardly. In Skinner's utopia we would learn systematically, using training exercises based on behaviourist principles. In a training exercise for children they are given a lollipop and told they can eat it later in the day, provided they do not lick it earlier; the lollipop is coated with powdered sugar so a supervisor can tell if it has been licked. The children are taught how to handle their frustration by putting the lollipop out of sight or by doing something to distract themselves. But since these kinds of solutions are not always available in real life, the exercise is later made harder by having the children wear the lollipops round their necks.

In one exercise the supervisor gradually reduces the amount of sugar in the children's cocoa until the drink tastes bitter. By then the children should have learnt to drink the unsweetened cocoa without pulling a face. In another exercise the children, coming in cold and hungry for supper, are made to wait five minutes with bowls of hot soup in front of them. At first they are allowed to talk and joke, but later they have to wait in silence so they can learn to cope on their own. The exercise is developed by dividing children into groups and deciding on the toss of a coin which sits and eats and which has to wait for five minutes.

Progress is monitored by supervisors and is discussed with the children. In this way they are prepared for the envy, frustration and jealousy of real life. It is particularly important that training should be based on rewarding good behaviour, not on punishing bad. The research of behaviourists has proved that reward is far more effective. Apart from being more effective, reward has other advantages over punishment. Put men in chains and beat them into building the pyramids, and the cost in terms of suffering and resentment is great. It will also be dangerous for the masters, since the slaves are likely to rebel. But when human beings do something for reward – even building a pyramid – they believe they are free and bear no resentment. Skinner's utopia need not be repressive in the way Freud thought all societies must be, because it is based on reward.

If a man mends a clock because you pay him well or he enjoys his work, he feels free. He is doing what he wants; doing what one wants, one feels free. According to Skinner, doing what one wants is only doing what one is rewarded for doing. In *Walden Two* people feel free because they are doing what they want, doing what they are rewarded for doing. In *Walden Two*, society is so arranged that when one does what others want, because it is rewarding for them, it is also what one wants to do oneself, because one is rewarded for doing it.

There is nothing remarkable, in Skinner's eyes, about a society that enables people to be happy. According to behaviourism, humans are pliable organisms with a handful of inborn reflexes and emotions, and a massive capacity to learn. What human beings become depends on the environment, which can shape them into almost any form. This is what makes utopia possible. 'Right conditions, that's all. Right conditions. All you need.' The words are those of Frazier, the fictional creator of Walden Two and Skinner's mouthpiece in the novel. From behaviourism we have learnt about rewards and the right conditions, and how the pliable organism each of us is at birth is shaped by experience. Pavlov's work with dogs provided the first clue.

Meat makes a hungry dog salivate, but the sound of a bell does not. In Pavlov's experiments, a bell was rung whenever a dog was given meat and then, after a number of times, the bell was rung without the meat being given. The dog salivated – at just the sound of the bell. The dog had learnt to salivate at the sound of a bell, by being rewarded with meat. This is classical conditioning. If Pavlov subsequently rang the bell a number of times without giving meat, the dog eventually stopped salivating at just the sound of the bell. According to behaviourism, this is largely how humans both learn and unlearn.

An early behaviourist experiment which achieved legendary status was J. B. Watson's study of Little Albert, a nine-month-old infant. A white rat was put beside Albert in the laboratory and he reached out for it, showing no sign of fear. While he was enjoying the rat's company and playing with it happily, Watson created a loud crash by striking an iron bar. Albert was startled and fell forward. This was repeated several times: Albert given the rat to play with, which he did happily, then the loud noise and Albert falling forward, startled. Soon Albert whimpered and showed signs of fear at the sight of the rat, before any noise was made. His fear persisted even after Watson stopped making the noise, and now Little Albert was frightened even by a white rabbit, a dog and a man's white beard. Eventually the effects wore off – they extinguished.

Parents have probably used reward and punishment in order to get children to do what they want since earliest times – with mixed results! What is new is behaviourism's systematic investigation of reward and punishment. What is also new is the conclusion behaviourists came to, that Pavlov's dogs and Watson's Little Albert provide an account of human beings. We start off with a handful of reflexes, a few emotions, and a capacity to learn. These, together with reward and punishment, explain human personality and behaviour. By means of reward and punishment we learn to build with toy bricks, ride a bicycle, speak, do sums, design a computer . . . behave in the way we behave and become what we are. Watson is on record as saying that, given a dozen healthy infants and the right conditions, he could turn any of them into doctor, lawyer, artist, merchant, beggar or thief.

Pavlov had to give his dogs meat to get them to salivate. In real life there is no Pavlov standing over us with meat to get us to do the right thing. What we do in real life – to start with – is haphazard. This is why, in Skinner's view, his work with pigeons gives a truer account of the human condition. What humans are really like is not Pavlov's dogs or Watson's Little Albert, but pigeons in a Skinner box.

A Skinner box is a cage containing a lever that releases food when it is pressed. A pigeon, put in a Skinner box, struts about till eventually it accidentally knocks the lever, and down comes the food, which it gobbles up. The pigeon continues to strut about until it hits the lever a second time and is rewarded with more food. This continues, with the times between the pigeon knocking the lever getting shorter and shorter. Eventually the pigeon stands by the lever, knocks it continuously and gobbles up the pellets as they fall. Skinner believes this operant conditioning explains all human behaviour that is not inherited. No God-like Pavlov with bits of meat is necessary to get some reaction because, like pigeons, humans are naturally active. What humans do is hit and miss at first, but eventually, like the pigeons, they do whatever they are rewarded for.

Behaviour therapy illustrates Skinner's operant conditioning. The therapist shows a dumb autistic child a cup and repeats 'cup' until the child says the word or makes a sound like it. If the child says 'cup' or something close, like 'cop' or 'tup', the therapist praises, caresses or gives the child a sweet. By rewarding the right sound or approximations and successive improvements, the therapist gets the child to learn several words. In a similar way the behaviour therapist works on a normal child or adult to eliminate phobias, aggression, obsessions. Behaviour therapy works because it ignores any supposed underlying causes and concentrates on behaviour. Phobias about spiders or dogs, criminal behaviour like stealing and rape, smoking, a tic, an obsession like Lady Macbeth's hand-washing, are not symptoms of any underlying conflict, as Freudian theory would have us believe. They are, according to behaviourism, just nasty habits which must be unlearnt and replaced by better habits.

Behaviour therapists are interested in behaviour not because behaviour is important but because – in their view – behaviour is all there is. Besides behaviour, and reward and punishment, there is nothing. If critics claim this is too simple an account of human beings, behaviourists reply that those who say this are ignorant of how complex reward and punishment can be.

Reward, whether praise, food or a caress, *pulls* behaviour in a certain direction, like a carrot. If a girl is praised or is successful when she confronts the class bully, she is more likely to confront the bully again. But though reward remains the best way, human behaviour can be shaped by other means. A riot policeman touches demonstrators squatting in the road with an electric prod and they get up and retreat. This is negative reinforcement and it *pushes* behaviour in a certain direction. A father grumbles at his son and stops only when the boy tidies his bedroom. The father's nagging makes the son tidy up his room because this puts a stop to the nagging. Negative reinforcement, the grumbling or electric shock, gets a son or demonstrator to do something to stop it – because 'it's nice when it stops'. Reward is like a carrot and negative reinforcement like an electric prod, but they are both to get people to do something. Punishment is different; it *stops* people doing something. The patient is given an electric shock when he has sexual feelings about children, not to make him do anything, but to stop him doing something – reacting sexually to children. This is the stick of punishment.

Reward works; the evidence of research is overwhelming. Encourage children to act aggressively and praise them when they hit a doll, and they will hit the doll hard and often. Suggest to children that they share their toys with other children, and shower them with praise or sweets when they do, and they will share their toys. Cue children into looking at their school books and reward them with attention when they do, and they will look at their school books. Children are not born aggressive or generous or studious, but they act aggressively, they share and they study when they are rewarded.

Much less effective than the carrot of reward is the electric prod of negative reinforcement. Negative reinforcement gets something done but not necessarily what the prodder wants. Demonstrators retreat before the riot squad, only to return later. What the riot squad really wanted was for the demonstrators to go away and not come back at all. The son may tidy his room because it is nice when the grumbling stops, but he may just walk out of the house. If he does, the grumbling has failed because it has not got what father wanted, a tidy room.

Just as negative reinforcement is not very effective in getting people to do things, so punishment is not very effective in stopping them. Smack a boy to stop him wiping his nose on his sleeve, and next time he may use his handkerchief or sniff, but he is just as likely to use his sleeve again. Punishment is not good at eliminating unwanted behaviour; it certainly does not connect a runny nose to using a handkerchief in the way that rewarding the boy for using a handkerchief would. Punishment connects nothing with nothing – but is not completely useless. It is used with some success in behaviour therapy to eliminate undesirable behaviour. A disturbed child bites and scratches himself, and a woman smokes non-stop. The behaviour therapist punishes or ignores the boy when he acts self-destructively; and he gives the smoker cigarettes which make her sick.

Reward is most effective if you receive it immediately, not after a long delay. How often you are rewarded is important. Some children were given a marble every time they hit a doll, others only occasionally. The children rewarded only occasionally were more aggressive and hit the dolls more often. When the marbles were stopped, the children who had been rewarded only occasionally went on being aggressive longer. Children and other animals learn quickly when they are rewarded every time but, as here with the marbles, they quickly stop once the rewards stop. Schedules of rewards vary in other ways. A weekly wage is regular but only occasional, as the employee is paid every seven days, not every five minutes or for every bit of work. When reward is tied to number, not to time, and the worker is paid for every bit of work, it is called piecework. The pieceworker is being rewarded for every washer (or whatever) produced, and pieceworkers paid by number of items usually work harder than those on a weekly wage. Like the pieceworkers, Skinner's pigeons pecked the lever more often when reward was based on number – that is, how often they did it – than when reward was based on time.

Animal research shows that rewards are more effective when given with some irregularity. The effectiveness of irregular rewards is also obvious in any pub where a fruit-machine or 'one-armed bandit' is being operated. Players continue pulling the lever long after they last won any money, just as the children, rewarded only occasionally, went on hitting dolls long after they last received a marble. Rewards that are irregular, not on a number basis like the one-armed bandit, but with regard to time, are also effective, as anyone waiting for a bus on an unreliable route knows. One waits for the bus with no idea when the next is likely to arrive, and goes on waiting, reasoning and hoping that a bus will arrive soon. This is the common-sense explanation, that rewards work, and irregular rewards work particularly well, because humans reason and think and hope. The punter continues to play the one-armed bandit, thinking his number must come up and that soon there will be the lovely crash of money in the tray. One goes on waiting at the bus-stop because one reasons that there must be a bus on the way somewhere.

But Skinner does not resort to explanations in terms of reasoning, thinking, hoping and other activities of a supposed mind. After all, irregular rewards prove very effective with pigeons. Pigeons can be made to work so hard with rewards varied by time that they consume more energy than they get from the occasional food-pellet. Quite literally they are working themselves to death. Pigeons do not use minds to reason and think and calculate the odds. So why, argues Skinner, should 'mind' be needed to explain human behaviour when the schedules of carrot, stick and electric prod are adequate?

There is a further complexity to pay-offs: they can be direct or indirect. 'In England they occasionally kill an admiral to encourage the rest,' claimed Voltaire. What effect does shooting one English admiral have on the others? Can carrot, stick and electric prod work at second hand, vicariously? In a typical experiment, children watch a film featuring attractive toys and two children, one of them very aggressive. In one version of the film the aggressive child ends up getting smacked and without the toys. In another version the aggressive boy ends up with the toys, which he has obtained by violence. It is always children who have seen the film where aggression pays off and gets the toys who are most aggressive in subsequent free-play situations. Children interviewed afterwards disapprove of the aggressive character, even those children who have just been imitating him. The evidence is clear: what matters is reward, and it can work indirectly and vicariously. Human beings learn to be aggressive, caring, sharing, attention-getting, dominating, supportive or selfish by seeing the aggressive, caring, sharing, attention-getting, dominating, supportive or selfish behaviour of others rewarded.

Vicarious reward is used in behaviour therapy to treat phobias. From a safe distance, a girl terrified of dogs watches another child playing with a dog. The child is obviously having fun with the dog, and during subsequent sessions the girl with the phobia is brought closer and closer. Eventually, as a result of the vicarious reward of the other child's obvious enjoyment, her phobia is overcome and she is able to play with the dog herself.

Another strand in the complex weave of reward, punishment and negative reinforcement is generalization and discrimination. A pigeon is trained in a Skinner box to peck a red lever for food. When the colour is gradually altered the pigeon continues pecking, but the more the colour shifts from the original red, the less the pigeon pecks, until eventually it stops. In another experiment, the colour of the lever is varied – sometimes red, sometimes green – and the pigeon is rewarded only when the lever is red. Eventually the pigeon pecks when the lever is red, but not when it is green. What has happened here is that with the introduction of only a slight complexity of rewards, the pigeon has learnt to generalize (different shades of red) and to discriminate (red, but not green). Behaviourists believe that a great deal of human learning happens this way, such as becoming masculine or feminine. A boy climbs trees, plays football, is assertive, competitive, because he is rewarded for 'masculine' activities. He learns not to play with dolls, Wendy houses and prams because these are punished with jeers and derision, or are negatively reinforced with disapproval which stops only when he goes off and kicks a football.

But the effects of pay-offs do not last for ever – extinction occurs. By pairing meat and bell, the dog learns to salivate at the sound of a bell. But if the bell is rung often enough without meat, the dog will stop salivating at just the bell. How quickly humans learn and unlearn varies, and there are inborn differences. Introverts condition more quickly and easily than extroverts, and their conditioning lasts longer once the pay-offs stop. In the behaviourist view criminals are likely to be people who condition to social rules slowly, with difficulty, and extinguish easily; these would be the extroverts. Research confirms that the majority of criminals tend to be extrovert.

But apart from a few inborn differences, such as introversion and extroversion, and the handful of reflexes and emotions we inherit in common, what makes personality is the carrot of reward, the stick of punishment and the electric prod of negative reinforcement. One person's reluctance to take risks and another's compulsion to gamble, one man's gentleness and another's toughness, one woman's tenderness with children and another's indifference, all these are the product of past and present pay-offs. They are nothing at all to do with any supposed internal forces such as Freud describes.

On Skinner's account, every human life is a kind of mini-evolution. In biological evolution random changes in genes, sifted by natural selection, caused the human species to emerge quite by chance. In a similar way every human life starts with actions that are random, like the mutating genes. Some of these hit-or-miss actions of human beings, like those of the pigeon in the Skinner box, have a pay-off from the environment and so survive. This survival of rewarded bits of behaviour is what makes us, just as in evolution the survival of the fittest eventually produced the human species. A zoologist wanting to explain the evolution of a turtle or of a two-humped camel studies the environment in which they evolved. What matters are the external conditions; and the same is true in each human life. There is no innate personality or human nature that causes us to do this or that. It is the other way around – we are made what we are by doing this and that. We are formed by the pay-offs of the environment, and particularly by reward. Those actions of ours that are rewarded become habits. Human nature is only habit.

So there is no innate, intractable and even nasty human nature for Skinner to contend with when it comes to creating his utopia. All that is needed for the good society and happy people are conditions that produce the right pay-offs. All that is needed is an environment where good behaviour is rewarded, and where only good behaviour is rewarded. But some thought has to be given to this since in the unplanned everyday world there are situations where bad behaviour is rewarded. While a child sits playing contentedly, his mother in the next room ignores him. If he breaks something or shouts angrily, his mother rushes in and rewards him with attention. Though mother wants less of breaking things and of angry shouting, this is what she rewards, so they are likely to increase. The contented playing which she wants more of she ignores, so it is likely to decrease.

It need not be like this. Society could be organized to ensure that only good behaviour is rewarded. Teachers, like the mother just described, often punish children when they should be rewarded and reward them when they should be punished. If children are working well teachers usually ignore them, but as soon as the children become noisy and disruptive teachers give them attention. In research, teachers have been helped to change to more appropriate pay-offs. An observer sits at the back of the class and when children are noisy, disruptive or not working, the observer cues the teacher to ignore them. When children are reading, playing well with others or working on a project, the observer cues teacher to go across and praise or encourage them. The results are that bad behaviour decreases and good behaviour increases.

But the observer cannot stay in the classroom for ever, cueing the teacher to what she should and should not do. It is not necessary. The teacher's new way of working itself rewards the teacher since it gets her what she wants: children behaving well; because of this, the teacher's new way of working will continue. If what happened in this classroom could become a model for society we would be on the way to utopia. 'Right conditions, that's all. Right conditions. All you need.' That is the perspective of Skinner's behaviourism.

Radical behaviourists regard their view of personality as the most scientific since it accounts for human behaviour – or attempts to – in terms of material causes. They avoid the idea that human behaviour is directed by purpose rather than by cause and effect, so there is nothing unscientific like free choice in its account. Nor is there the faintest trace of a non-material ghost in the machine since mind is an illusion and only the physical is real. But the supposedly most scientific account of personality most contradicts common sense. Unlike the other theories, radical behaviourism cannot work alongside and supplement common sense; it can only supplant it. And despite its scientific pretensions, many of the central concepts of behaviourism, such as reward, reinforcement, generalization, remain vague and ill-defined.

Skinner's experimental work has been original and brilliant, but can a perspective on human beings be derived from research with rats and pigeons? Other behaviourists have worked with children. But even generalizing to the adult world from laboratory data on children watching films and hitting dolls is stretching a point. Perhaps all laboratory research, be it with children or adults, is of doubtful relevance as human life takes place in society, not in a culture-free laboratory. Human life in the real world is surrounded by values and attitudes and laws and beliefs. No anthropologist would talk about Eskimos or members of the Kikuyu tribe without first explaining their society and its culture. In his more social version of behaviourism, Mead regarded laboratory research as pointless for this very reason – humans can be understood only in their social situation.

Mead's social behaviourism stresses that in real life we relate to brothers, friends, parents, the milkman, wives ... not to objects like toys and dolls and levers and mazes. Do rats or pigeons sit down at certain places at the table when they eat, wait (sometimes) for everyone to be served, have a certain order of courses, and perhaps even say grace? Does the rat or pigeon care who it mates with? But radical behaviourists like Skinner ignore values, choices, hopes and purposes in human life, believing that, since these are subjective, they are entitled to ignore them or explain them away. But such subjective experiences are central to being human, and it seems pointless to pretend otherwise.

Freud is uncertain whether human behaviour is wholly caused, or only partially caused so leaving a degree of freedom, but he is certain that those causes are within. For Freud the causes of our actions are internal bodily instinct, only slightly affected by external experience. Skinner is certain that human behaviour is completely caused and that those causes are external, the pay-offs of the environment. Skinner is a hard determinist, arguing that the idea of human beings having free choice is a myth. It is only because the causes of human action are hidden in the environment that the myth survives. When what we do is dictated by force or the threat of force, it is obvious to everyone that we are not free. A man wants to steal or rape but the possibility of prison stops him. There is no free choice here, merely behaviour constrained by the threat of imprisonment. The punishment or negative reinforcement of prison, beatings, handcuffs, violence leaves us in no doubt that we are being coerced. But with reward we have seen it is possible to retain the illusion that we are free.

A housewife standing before a kitchen sink full of dirty clothes thinks she is free – to wash or not to wash. But the housewife is as much tied to the sink by the pile of clothes as a convict held by a chain to the rocks he is breaking. What holds her – the reward of a job well done, her husband's thanks, her children's smart appearance – is different from and less obvious than the manacles of a chain gang. In Skinner's view, she is nevertheless completely bound to the kitchen sink.

Skinner contends that the illusion of freedom is at its most powerful when what we do is caused by reward, like the woman at the sink or a monk in a monastery. A monk responds to bells with a speed that puts Pavlov's dogs to shame: bells that tell him to rise in the morning, that make him start chanting, that make him speak or stay silent, that get him to the refectory and eating, to his study and reading, to the farm and working, to the dormitory and sleeping. The monk's reactions were originally shaped by reward in his early novice years, but he is still rewarded now. The monk may delude himself that he is free because – he will argue – he does not have to stay in the monastery; he chose to be a monk and nothing prevents him walking out now. Certainly neither force nor the threat of force stops him leaving, but what does is past and present pay-offs. The rewards of the environment shape not only behaviour but motives, desires and wishes that incline us to behave. As a child, his Catholic parents trained him in Christian habits, the Catholic school shaped his practices, the priests in the parish moulded his behaviour. The rewards of the past brought the monk into the monastery and, interacting with his past, the rewards of the present keep him there now. The monk is more like the woman tied to the kitchen sink than the convict but, in Skinner's view, he is no free agent.

What the monk does is caused by past and present pay-offs, but he believes he is free because they are inconspicuous. And he believes he is free because he is doing what he 'wants', and doing what one wants is 'being free'. But, as we have seen, doing what one wants is simply doing what one is rewarded for doing. No one physically constrains Mrs Smith to stay at home and be a housewife, and no material force or threat compels Brother John to remain in the monastery, responding to the bells. They do it because they want to, and they want to because this is what they are rewarded for. Failing to see the causes of their behaviour, our housewife and monk feel that they are free because they are doing what they 'want'; but they are only doing what they are rewarded for doing. Behaviourists contend that, with their knowledge of the way in which the environment shapes the behaviour of men and women, they have in be-haviourism a scientific explanation of human actions, and free choice has no place in it.

But despite the ingenuity of the argument Skinner and the radical behaviourists are wrong. The situation of monk and housewife is different from that of the man in prison or chains. The behaviour of housewife and monk may be shaped and modified by its pay-offs, but it is not completely determined by them. Housewives do take off their aprons and leave the kitchen sink, and monks do walk out of monasteries.

The behaviourist reply is that when they do, there must be

other pay-offs which make leaving the sink or the monastery more rewarding than staying. Once this is said, and it is the only behaviourist answer to apparent free choices, what seemed a scientific account begins to look more like faith. When someone appears to make a choice, such as to quit the kitchen sink or the monastery, the behaviourist simply says that what appears to be free only does so because we have failed to discover what the real pay-offs were. We are back to a 'Heads I win, tails you lose' situation, as with Freud's repression. At least the opposite assertion, of a modest degree of free choice, has the advantage of having common sense and human experience on its side.

For Freud no utopia is possible, and human society is for ever in danger of degenerating into a jungle where only the strongest survive. Utmost vigilance is necessary because, whatever else humans may be, they are dangerous. But Skinner sees things differently; according to his view humans start off neither dangerous nor caring and loving, but as pliable plasticine for the fingers of reward and punishment to shape. Humans are not born violent and aggressive, but they act violently and aggressively if that is what they are rewarded for. Humans are not caring and kind because this is how they are born, but because this is what they were rewarded for in the past and still are now. Helping others, acting honestly and telling the truth are not the result of some internal Freudian super-ego. Cheating, hurting others, rape and murder are not our chosen disobedience to a moral law. Whether we are a help to others or a danger depends quite simply on what we are rewarded and punished for. 'Good' and 'bad' are the result of right and wrong reinforcement by the environment.

It is clear what is meant by being a help to others or being dangerous. Are good and bad just this? Yes, in Skinner's view, more or less. In *Beyond Freedom and Dignity* he states: 'Behaviour is called good or bad . . . according to the way in which it is usually reinforced by others.' Stop at the traffic lights if they are red, and drive on if they are green. Spelt out in greater detail, this is saying: if you cross the lights when they are red someone will crash into you, but stop and you will be safe; if you cross the lights when they are green you will cross safely, but if you stop someone will hoot at you or crash into your rear. Motorists should obey these rules for their own good. If they do, they will be rewarded with safe crossings and undamaged cars; if they do not, they will be punished with crashes and the anger of others and even loss of life. Good and bad are no different from these rules. If you help others, you will be rewarded with thanks or with help in return; if you hurt someone, you will be punished with a spell in prison or with being hurt yourself. In Skinner's account, good and bad are what others reward and punish us for.

Life is like driving. If we spell out moral codes and the good and bad which all societies have, we find that they are no different from Highway Codes and the rules for good and bad driving. Humans are not moral, and our behaviour is good when it is rewarding to others, and our behaviour is bad when others find it punishing. 'Good' behaviour is what others reward us for doing, and they reward us because our behaviour is rewarding to them. My kindness helps you, so you call it good and reward me in return. My dishonesty is 'bad' because others punish me for it, and they punish me because my dishonesty is punishing to them. In Western society few stars are awarded to a prostitute, more to an unmarried mother who does a decent job, many to a successful career woman or a good wife and mother, and to a woman who combines a career with being a good wife and mother, any number of stars – and gold ones at that.

Skinner believes that there is no internal moral dimension; there is nothing moral and nothing internal. When I learn to drive I start with an instructor who rewards me with praise for getting the gears right. But I do not end up internalizing my instructor in the way I internalize Father or Mother to form a Freudian super-ego. Eventually the carrot of reward, the electric prod of negative reinforcement and the stick of punishment are administered by the environment, not by my instructor. If I get the gears wrong, they crash or the car shudders and stalls; this is my punishment. If I get the gears right, I am rewarded with a smooth drive. What controls my behaviour is not an internal instructor but the externals of the smooth drive or the discomfort and danger of getting it wrong. There is no such thing as morality, either inside humans or outside in society; there is only mutual reinforcement. If we could arrange the reinforcement right, we would have utopia!

But who is to arrange the right rewards and punishments to create Skinner's utopia, and to decide how many stars are appropriate and which should be gold? In Dostoevsky's 'Legend of the Grand Inquisitor' in *The Brothers Karamazov*, society is planned and controlled by an elite who decide what everyone should do. They hold on to their own freedom while the rest give up theirs. But in Skinner's utopia not only are good and bad an illusion, but freedom and choice are too. Since freedom and choice are an illusion, it is baffling how in Skinner's utopia the planners can plan, since one has to be free in the first place to be able to plan.

And Skinner's view that morality is like the Highway Code seems plainly inadequate. 'I ought to indicate clearly when about to turn left' and 'I ought not to brake without warning the driver behind' do state what one *ought* to do. But these *oughts* are different from those of 'I ought to care about my ageing parents' and 'I ought not seduce my best friend's wife'. The first two *oughts* are practical guidelines, and some (like driving on the left) are mere conventions. But the second set of *oughts* – the ones common sense calls morals – bind in a different way and are not local, like driving on the left. All societies say one ought to care for one's parents, though this caring takes different forms. All societies assert that one ought not betray the trust of certain people, like seducing the wife of a best friend. As we shall see, for Carl Rogers there is a universal moral dimension which is part of human nature, and which is nothing like the Highway Code or rules for good driving. This is also the common-sense view.

Finally, there is the question of mind. Skinner and the radical behaviourists believe that mind, consciousness and the I are illusion. Like Freud, behaviourists are materialists for whom only the physical is real. But Freud knows that mind exists, though he cannot explain it. For radical behaviourists mind is only illusion to be explained away; what exists is behaviour and nothing more. We do not resort to mystical concepts like mind or a conscious I to explain the pigeon's behaviour in a Skinner box. Learning to press a lever, even choosing a special colour, might once have passed for pigeon thinking, but now we have no difficulty in explaining them in terms of rewards and reinforcement. If we can explain away the workings of pigeon-mind in this way, argues Skinner, why not human mind?

A man lunges at me with a knife, and I am frightened and run. Common sense says I run because I am frightened and common sense says that something in the mind like fear causes bodily behaviour like running. Skinner says it is the other way around. When the man lunges at me with a knife, my heart beats faster and stronger, my glands secrete hormones, my breathing speeds up. Fear is the experience of these bodily reactions. The man lunging is a negative reinforcement, so I run away to make it stop. The fear is as physical as the running, and both are rewarded by the man being out of sight or in the distance. There is no mind responsible for anything going on; there is only behaviour, some of it verbal, and reward and punishment and negative reinforcement.

If some children had been around when the man lunged and I had stayed and confronted him, my courage would have been praised, as if courage was something stored in me like infor-mation in a computer. But I would have stayed and confronted him only because I was rewarded by the sight of safe children. This in brief is Skinner's explanation – or explaining away – of mind. But one question will not disappear: who or what is experiencing the heart beating faster, the secretion of glands, the speeded-up breathing, and even the fear? Common sense calls it the 'I'.

For Skinner, the I and the mind are only old ghosts from an outdated way of thinking, with the scientific value of a ghost story. There is only a machine called the brain. Behaviour is the result of reward, negative reinforcement and punishment, which research will eventually show are electrical impulses and chemi-cal activity of brain and nervous system.

Behaviourists concede that the activities of so-called mind, though an illusion, remain a powerful illusion. The deception, they contend, arises from our use of language – the myth of mind and the I exists because of the way we talk. We are misled into thinking that mind and the I exist because we cling to archaic words like 'thinking', 'remembering', 'feeling', 'deciding'. We insist on clinging to outmoded language from a pre-scientific age, even though we no longer talk about goblins, demons and angels. Speak a dead language and you are stuck with dead ideas. Talk properly about nerves, cells, brain and behaviour, and mind will disappear like demons, witches, goblins and fairies at the bottom of the garden. As research progresses, particularly brain research, the biologist's language of cell function, nerve activity and brain processes will integrate with the psychologist's talk of reinforcement and behaviour to produce a scientific explanation. Nonsense words create the nonsense of mind and the I. When we adopt the right scientific language we will see there are only brain states and behaviour and will recognize thinking, remembering, feeling, deciding for what they are . . . illusion.

Language certainly shapes the way we . . . think! If we talk differently about mind, we will 'think' differently about 'mind' . . . or rather we will 'have different cell activity about brain'. But thoughts, memories, feelings, decisions are as real as death and taxes; and like death and taxes they will not go away if we stop talking about them. The suggestion that we will see mind as an illusion when we talk differently about mind is an attempt to rescue an absurd position. It is materialism on promise, and it is nonsense because our common sense knows that the activities of mind are real. There is no way in which we can ignore the reality of our experience of thoughts, memories, feelings, decisions. No matter how far research advances understanding of the brain's mechanisms, the reality of our subjective experience is not going to disappear. There are two levels, brain and mind; and brain research or talking differently about them is not likely to dispense with the reality of either. The behaviourist position is ingenious but absurd.

Skinner's account may be right with other animals. In his research with rats and pigeons he has been able to eliminate all the complex factors that affect human behaviour. But there is an observable hierarchy of complexity in living organisms, and it is unlikely that something more complex will behave in the same way (only more so) as something less complex. The complex human being has to be explained in terms of its own complexity. Species-specific features of human beings, such as language and thought and culture, call for species-specific explanations. This seems more scientific than saying, with Skinner, that human beings are nothing but pigeons only more so ... more intelligent, better at learning, with greater memories. The attempt to explain human personality should be concerned not only with those features we share with rats and pigeons but also, even primarily, with those features which other animals do not have and which are more or less exclusively human.

Common sense recognizes a problem in thinking and feeling and fearing and hoping and deciding and seeing yellow, but it is a problem to be solved, not an illusion. It is not only common sense that acknowledges the reality of the raw experience of fear and thinking and the fight-or-flight decision. Most other theories of personality, though uncertain as to what mind and its activities and the I are, remain confident that they exist.

It is significant that cognitive psychology, which emphasizes activities of the mind such as thinking, remembering, attention, language, is now replacing behaviourism. Also significant are changes within the behaviourist tradition, associated with Albert Bandura and others, which recognize cognitive factors. It is now realized that rewards and punishment may work because we anticipate and expect them, and 'anticipation' and 'expectation' are activities of mind. Our earlier examples of the housewife and the monk illustrate this. No one may actually thank or reward either housewife or monk for what they do, but what they do is rewarding for them because of the way they see the situation. It is when the woman no longer *sees* her domestic tasks as rewarding that she decides to return to her career. If the monk loses his faith and no longer *believes*, then the monastic chores become just chores and no longer his path to God, and he leaves the monastery.

But these cognitive factors were always around, even in the most mind-less behaviourism. The research, where the film of a boy rewarded for being aggressive made the watching children aggressive, is given as evidence for the effectiveness of reward. But the same research also supports the reality of internal mental activities. The children experience the effectiveness of reward vicariously – watching the film – only if they can imaginatively take the role of the aggressive boy in the film and identify with him. Imaginatively taking the role and identifying are activities of mind. The pigeon may go on pressing the lever because of past reinforcement, but human beings partly go on waiting for a bus because they *expect* one to turn up. Expecting is mental activity again. What is becoming clear is that how people *see* a situation, with its rewards, punishments and pay-offs, is mental activity and is important, just as common sense had always thought.

But the contribution of Skinner and other radical behaviourists is not to be ignored. Anthropologists have made us aware how our personalities and behaviour are shaped by culture. Feminists point out how girls are made feminine and boys masculine by the pressures of society. We shall see that role theorists and G. H. Mead reveal the power of social class to affect us. But neither anthropologist, nor feminist, nor the more social accounts spell out the mechanisms by which this is done. Behaviourism attempts to do just that. Behaviourism proposes schedules of reward, punishment and negative reinforcement, both direct and vicarious, as the mechanisms by which such shaping of our personality and behaviour takes place. Behaviourism goes on to argue with some evidence that reward, punishment and negative reinforcement, in the past and present, cause our aggression or docility, our studiousness or lack of studiousness, our racial prejudice, moral concern, kindness, bullying, care of others, wife-battering . . . We are what we are because of conditioning by the environment.

Even in education and skills training, behaviourism has made a contribution. For example, it has made us aware of the importance of breaking down learning tasks into manageable units, of guidance to ensure that the learner carries out the right actions, of practice, and particularly of practice with reinforcement. Similarly, behaviourist ideas are the basis for teaching men and women how to assert themselves legitimately in what is called assertiveness training. Skinner's principles of learning have been used as a basis for techniques of teaching people with learning difficulties such as mental handicap. Finally, the behaviourism of Skinner and others has provided the principles for behaviour therapy. Phobias, tics, compulsions, sexual inhibitions, obsessions, self-destructive acts are all treated by behaviour therapy, and many sufferers have been and are still being relieved of the distress these cause.

But human beings are not empty organisms, nor are they merely plasticine creatures which the rewards, punishment and negative reinforcement of external circumstances totally form. Human beings are shaped by their environment, but in turn they shape their environment – this is the view of Mead's social behaviourism as well as of common sense. The remarkable transformation of the world wrought by humans might with ingenuity be accounted for – in theory – by behaviourism, but the explanation stretches belief. Human life is characterized by language, culture, science, technology, religion, the arts and a whole variety of other complex activities which no one has yet observed in a pigeon. Skinner's explanation may be adequate for rats and pigeons, but the complexity of human behaviour cannot be accounted for only in terms of conditioning. The common-sense view that human beings are born with innate capacities and inclinations seems more likely. Human beings are not completely plasticine at birth, as any parent will tell you. Skinner's account of human beings as high-grade pigeons contradicts common sense, but the radical behaviourist perspective remains ingenious and is not to be completely dismissed.

Chapter Four

FLOWER PEOPLE:
Carl Rogers' self theory

To thine own self be true.

Shakespeare: *Hamlet*, Act I, sc. iii

For Skinner there is little more to human beings than behaviour, but for Rogers there is also the self. The self has a long history; for thousands of years the great religions have urged their followers: 'Know thy*self*' . . . 'Love your neighbour as your*self*'. The self is to be found in everyday common-sense language: 'John is not his usual cheerful *self* these days' . . . 'I don't really see my*self* as a teacher'. Modern psychology and particularly behaviourism discarded the self since it was invisible, vague and – it was felt – a shade mystical.

But if the self seemed too ghostly for scientific psychologists, it felt real enough to the people who went to Carl Rogers and other counsellors for help. 'Since the children left home I've been depressed, not my old self at all.' 'I put on an act with people – I can't be my real self with them.' Rogers' account of the self and personality can best be understood through his approach to counselling and therapy.

Janet attends the student health unit. Work, college, boyfriend, parents, in fact life generally, have been getting too much for her, and she feels depressed, anxious, dissatisfied. Others might struggle dutifully on but Janet, like the flower people, believes that feeling good is important. She wants to live a fulfilled life, which is why she has come for counselling. When counselling began Janet was encouraged to talk, and the therapist listened sympathetically. 'I haven't been feeling myself recently,' Janet said. 'I pretend to be cheerful at college but it's really an act . . . Since I split up with Michael I'm not sure of myself any more . . . A couple of tutors have complained about my work recently . . . I don't understand myself and what I want.' What becomes clear is the importance of how she sees her-*self*.

How each of us see himself or herself is not only important in its own right, it affects what we do. If I see myself as a devout Catholic, I will attend mass regularly. If I see myself as a conscientious employee, I will arrive at work on time and rarely be absent. People even choose jobs that go with the way they see themselves, as a risk-taking salesman, say, rather than a cautious bank clerk. Most of what we do is an attempt to be consistent with the way we see ourselves. Human behaviour, in Carl Rogers' view, is a product of the self.

After twenty sessions Janet is talking differently: 'I don't seem so mixed up about myself . . . I'm beginning to get a better view of myself.' Not only has the way she sees herself changed, but her behaviour has changed too. 'I've turned in better college work recently . . . I don't always pretend now that I'm cheerful when I'm not . . . I got in touch with Michael recently to talk things over.' Her behaviour has changed not because of the unconscious becoming conscious, as Freud would contend. Nor is she acting differently because of a different pattern of reward and punishment, as Skinner would argue. Her behaviour has changed because her self has changed. Behaviour is a product of the self, and when the self changes, behaviour changes too. What changes first in therapy is how we see things, particularly how we see our self. Once we see our self differently, we act differently. This is the basis for Rogerian counselling.

Rogers has called his approach 'non-directive therapy'. What a fly on the wall would see is Janet talking while the therapist listens, shows interest, smiles, makes encouraging noises, occasionally offers a comment or interpretation. But the therapist does nothing that would direct what Janet thinks, feels, says. Rogers has also called his therapy 'person-centred' to emphasize that what matters is a relationship, not to a client or to a patient but to a person.

Rogers has described his therapy as 'short term' since he

believed that improvement is possible in months rather than years. The self is not a solid structure to be chipped away at, like a sculptor working in marble or stone. Improvement can happen quickly because the self is dynamic; it is an awareness that can alter over a short period. Just as the sketch artist's pencil turns a sad face into a happy one with a few lines, so in therapy the awareness that makes up the self can be changed with just a few touches.

What becomes clear to the therapist is that Janet is a house divided against it*self*. She is fond of her parents, likes Michael, and enjoys her studies. Janet is aware of this, but there are other feelings that she is not aware of or able to admit to. She also feels angry with her parents for pressuring her into going to polytechnic when she might have preferred a job, money and travel. She is fond of Michael but is reluctant to commit herself in the relationship; and though finding her studies interesting she resents having to live off a meagre student grant.

On the one hand there is what she feels and admits to feeling; on the other, there is what she feels but refuses to admit. The result is a discrepancy between what the self feels and what it admits to feeling – hence the house (or self) divided against itself. Rogers calls this 'incongruence', and it is why Janet feels depressed, anxious, dissatisfied. A man sees himself as having an enlightened respect for women but is unaware of the contempt he also feels, which is why he has phobias. A woman regards herself as gentle but frequently feels a violence she will not recognize and, as a result, is often depressed. The origins of such divisions usually go back to childhood.

The little girl opens her magic painting book, wipes the empty page with a damp cloth, and a picture emerges. Each of us begins life like the blank page in the painting book, and our experience brings out the picture. But Rogers' empty page is different from Skinner's pliable plasticine or the blank slate of Mead's social behaviourism. As we shall see in Chapter Six, there really is nothing on social behaviourism's blank slate at the start, and what eventually appears is only what the finger of experience writes. But there is already a picture on Rogers' empty page, though it is hidden and needs experience to reveal it. What is there on the page waiting to be revealed by the damp cloth of experience is the self.

A baby begins life surrounded by buzzing and booming experiences. Baby is eventually able to organize and make sense of this confusion of experience and to react to it. But experience is always what the baby and, later, the child and adult react to. Whatever the real world 'out there' is really like, all that any of us can ever know and react to is our experience of the world. It is always a question of experience, and a key area of experience is the self. Definitions of the self, such as Rogers', refer to an awareness of the I and Me, and of their relationship to others and the world.

Janet's parents loved her as a child but there were always strings attached to their love. When a younger brother arrived Janet resented the attention he received, envied him, often wanted to kick him, and occasionally did. As a child Janet was sometimes angry and assertive. But her parents loved her only if she did not envy and kick her brother and was not angry and assertive. Needing their love Janet developed a self that her parents would approve of, one without envy, resentment, anger, assertiveness or an inclination to kick her brother. She denied and distorted what she really felt – and this, in Rogers' view, is when the self divides against itself.

What happened to Janet happens to most of us because parents usually lay down certain conditions for their love. They will love and value us only if we stop hitting our brother, stop breaking things, stop defecating where we please. With some parents it is not enough that we do the right thing. We also have to feel the right thing. It is not enough to stop kicking our brother – we must stop wanting to kick him or envying him all the attention he gets. It is not enough to stop breaking things or defecating when and where we please, we must stop even wanting to. We end up denying and distorting those experiences our parents disapprove of; we end up, according to Rogers, disowning part of our self.

There may be a picture of our true self hidden in the blank page but, like Janet's, the self that emerges may be distorted by our experience. Rogers believes that if the self is to emerge healthy and sound we need to be loved and valued without strings. If our self is to develop without distortion, we need to know that our being there makes a difference to others, and that they do not mind what our self is like. If we are loved and valued in this unconditional way, we can advance to loving and valuing ourselves in such a way. When Captain Oates walked out into the Antarctic snow, it was the love and respect he had for himself, as much as his concern for others, that triumphed over the desire to survive.

Rogers believes that if our early experience were one of being loved unconditionally, we would emerge from childhood healthy and full of self-respect. Unfortunately we rarely grow up valuing ourselves enough since we have rarely been valued enough by others. Our experience, like Janet's, is more likely to have stunted and distorted the growth of our personality, and from the damp cloth of experience a flawed self emerges.

If the love we received as children was without strings, personality development would be healthy. Parents need not approve of everything a child feels and says and does, but they should approve unconditionally of the child. If they did, children could accept themselves as they are, and the self would emerge whole. Janet's parents could disapprove of her kicking her brother – for little brother's sake, if for no other! – but still love Janet completely. Then there would be no need for Janet to deny and distort what she really felt. But since this was not the way Janet's childhood was, what will help her now? Rogers lists three conditions that are necessary for change in therapy.

First, a therapist can create an atmosphere which makes change possible only if she is herself sorted out. In situation comedies, 'agony aunts' sort out other people's problems while failing to solve their own. But only a therapist who has a genuine self, is trusting and is not on the defensive – Rogers calls all this 'congruence' – can offer Janet a real relationship which will help her grow. (This is true also of the parent–child relationship. How can we help our children sort themselves out if we are mixed up ourselves?)

Secondly, if Janet is to get her self together she needs to feel that the therapist accepts her as she is – she needs love without strings. Rogers calls this 'unconditional positive regard'. It was the conditional, strings-attached love of Janet's parents that damaged her self in the first place. The therapist must be able to care about Janet even if she expresses hateful prejudices and opinions, or even if the way she treated Michael seems cruel. Sensing this positive caring attitude Janet feels: 'If the therapist can accept me as I am, so can I.' This makes change possible. It is a paradox of human psychology that only when someone (therapist, parent, wife, husband) accepts one as one is, is it possible to change and become something different.

Thirdly, for Janet to make progress the therapist must be able to get inside her frame of reference and feel with her. The therapist must be able, for example, to see the relationship with Michael the way Janet does, as pleasurable but imprisoning, and be able to experience her anger with her parents. The therapist must be able to feel 'empathy' and convey the empathy to Janet.

In therapy and in life what is needed for humans to grow and develop, for change to be possible, is a relationship in which another person provides these three conditions: genuineness or congruence, a love that is unconditional or without strings, and empathy. If they are present, humans will move in the direction of fulfilment because there is a force for growth within us. Humans have a master motive – to live fulfilled lives. There exists in us all a tendency to develop, to actualize and use our capacities and potential to the full. This was Rogers' belief, based on his experience as a therapist. We want to grow and lead rich fulfilled lives, like the flower people but without the drugs and the irresponsibility, since our place is in the driving seat. If bad experience has displaced us, the task of therapy is to put us back in the driving seat.

Janet's father could not bear anyone to be sad and gloomy about the house; like any other child, however, Janet had her low times. She was particularly depressed when her grandparents died; but her father, having his own grief to cope with, would not allow Janet to be sad even then. As her father would love her only if she was cheerful, Janet was cheerful. Some of her experience, the sad and depressed bit, she could not afford to admit to as part of herself since it risked losing her father's love.

When she and Michael separated, the sadness she felt was not acceptable to her cheerful, father-approved-of self, so she denied the feeling and smiled bravely on. But sadness or anger or envy do not disappear because we do not admit to them. We still feel sad, depressed, angry and envious without being aware that we do. This 'discernment without awareness' Rogers calls subception. Discerning a feeling without being fully aware, as Janet did in her sadness at Michael leaving, is threatening. If she were to admit to the sadness her self would be at risk. With her cheerful, father-approved-of self under threat from sadness, it is no wonder she felt anxious and unable to cope!

How does Janet defend against experiences she dare not admit to? According to Rogers, she denies or distorts them. Denial is a defence we adopt in order to protect ourselves from unacceptable truths by refusing to see them. 'I'm really rather relieved Michael has gone – we were always arguing ... I feel sorry for students who always get good marks – they must spend all their time working.' With distortion we alter the experience to make it acceptable. 'Michael and I haven't split up – we're having a trial separation ... I wasn't putting on an act at the party – I was joking to make everyone laugh.'

In the medieval legend an artist is given two commissions: one to paint a picture of Christ as a child, the other to paint the devil. He looks for models, finds a child with an innocent face, and paints the young Christ. But he fails to find what he wants for his portrait of the devil and abandons the commission. Years later he discovers the corrupt, degraded face he was looking for all that time before, and paints his picture of the devil. It is the same person who sat for the earlier painting.

What Rogers believes is that each of us enters the world with potential for growth and, given the right soil, healthy growth will occur. But an environment where love is conditional on our feeling a certain way is the wrong soil; such an environment distorts the self and puts our personality on the defensive. To the extent that this defensiveness succeeds we have a rigid personality, distorting what it sees and unable to acknowledge reality and ourselves as they really are. If the defence fails we have outright anxiety. In either case the situation is one of maladjustment, and the feelings, behaviour and defence mechanisms of neurosis come into play: projection, compulsions, depression, phobias, rationalization, obsession.

But there is another, more healthy type of soil where children receive love without strings. Loved and valued unconditionally by parents, they do not have to disown any of their feelings and experiences but can accept them all as part of themselves. Human beings have only to be loved and valued without strings, by the therapist in therapy, or by parents, lover, friend, wife or husband in everyday life. The result is the fully functioning person, Rogers' picture of mental health and the good life. The fully functioning person is Rogers' account of how human beings ought to be, like Freud's genital personality. There are three important features of such a personality.

First, the fully functioning person is open to experience. No longer a house divided against itself, the individual is aware of his or her own anger as well as love, sexuality besides tenderness, envy as much as compassion. Once the less positive aspects are accepted, they cease to be damaging. The anger, raw sexuality and envy work healthily once admitted to self. With harmony between self and experience, it is possible for the person to be open and to accept new experiences. The self can afford to be open because it has nothing to hide or be on the defensive about. Secondly, the fully functioning personality is alive in the present, in the here and now; he or she lives existentially. With no straitjacket imposed on experience, such a personality explores the exciting possibilities of every new moment. Thirdly, the fully functioning personality trusts his or her own reactions. What feels right does so because it has proved to be a good guide in the past and will probably be so in the future. Being open and alive to the present ensures that the person recognizes the relevance of what is going on. For this reason, fully functioning people have no need for rules, commandments or gurus to guide them. Their own experience is the most reliable signpost to what they should do.

Criticisms of Rogers' therapy serve also to criticize his account of personality since the two relate closely. He has been called the 'mmm-hmm' psychologist, because Rogerian therapists are expected to sit making encouraging 'mmm-hmm' noises in therapy but not to be directive. Behaviourists argue that such supposedly non-directive therapists direct, without realizing, by rewarding the words and reactions they approve of with smiles, nods and encouraging 'mmm-hmm' noises. By not responding at all, therapists are punishing or negatively reinforcing clients when they speak or react in a way the therapists do not approve of. There is some evidence to support this interpretation and to suggest that 'non-directive' therapists do direct and shape behaviour in this way. This would mean, in behaviourist terms, that Rogerian therapy is merely an inefficient form of conditioning and behaviour therapy. For behaviourists, Rogers is talking nonsense in claiming that human beings are in the driving seat and in control of their own lives.

Rogers' emphasis on the self again puts him at odds with the behaviourists who regard with suspicion anything that smacks of mind. He diverges from them further in placing so little emphasis on behaviour. 'I used to see my*self* as boring, and I was always shy at parties. Therapy made me see my*self* as interesting and stimulating and gave me confidence.' According to Rogers, behaviour is a product of the self and if the self changes behaviour changes too. But the behaviourists point out that I may now go to parties with my new improved self and still not know how to introduce myself to strangers, initiate conversation, be entertaining, react with interest to what others say. What is important, according to behaviourism, is learning the right behaviour and appropriate social skills; but Rogers' emphasis on how we see the world and our selves ignores this.

Rogers differs from Freud in giving very little place to the unconscious. Subception, knowing without awareness, is only a modest form of unconscious activity. Since the theory emphasizes what we experience, and the unconscious is in some sense what we do not experience, the unconscious can play only a small part in such an account.

Is love without strings really possible – other than with a

baby? A woman discovers a friend to be an active racist; the therapist realizes that a man coming for counselling molests children; Janet, now in her teens, persists in ridiculing her brother to his face. Is it possible for the woman, the therapist, the parents to love now without placing conditions on their love? Rogers claims that one can draw a distinction between a person and his or her views, feelings and deeds – and he has respectable antecedents for this claim. In the New Testament, Christ speaks of coming 'to condemn sin but not the sinner'. Perhaps Rogerian therapy works – and this is not to belittle it – like the best kind of conversion experience. I approach with my sins and guilt, and God – or the therapist – loves me as I am, warts and all, sin and guilt. If God or the therapist can accept me as I am, so can I. Accepting myself as I am – we are back to the paradox – makes it possible to become a new person, which is what therapy and conversion are about.

Rogers does not ignore the force of raw emotion. But in the Rogerian account of personality what we recognize is flower-power, the best type of hippie in ourselves, the desire for peace, love and understanding and to live the good life. Where is the Freudian creature of sexuality, violence, self-interest and passion that we read about daily in the tabloids and are aware of in ourselves? And perhaps there is no inborn master-motive, no drive to live fulfilled lives. Why humans do anything at all may be, as Freud and Fromm assert, because of the gulf between what we need and what circumstances provide.

What is Rogers' solution to the body-mind problem? I go to the doctor and complain of a pain in my leg and of feeling depressed. For the doctor, the pain in my leg has to do with my body and the depression with my mind. But to me, his distinction is largely irrelevant. *I* am suffering. It is not my body that has a pain in its leg, not my mind that has a depression – I do. The pain and the depression are what I experience; and staying with my experience, the body–mind distinction becomes irrelevant. Body exists, and low blood-sugar may be an element in my depression. But the only reality for any of us is our experience, which makes little distinction between body and mind. Rogers does not solve the body–mind problem but he avoids it by sticking to experience.

So what is this conscious person which experiences? What is this 'I' that feels pain in the leg and suffers from depression? Skinner regards anything to do with mind as illusion. Freud regards mind as very real but does not know what it is. Rogers sides with Freud and common sense in regarding the mind and I as a fact of everyone's experience which cannot be denied and which needs to be accounted for.

For Rogers, a clue as to how conscious I originates is to be found in therapy, where time and again he has observed people striving to live fulfilled lives. Rogers believes that what he has observed in therapy is one expression of a tendency at work in the universe. All living things, whether trees, potatoes or humans, struggle to fulfil their potential. The plant strives upwards to find sunlight and stretches outwards for nourishment in the soil. This endeavour to find fulfilment is present throughout evolution, in the movement from the simple to the complex, from gases to galaxies, from amoeba to primates. In evolution the process has reached its high point with the emergence of the human I.

The idea of a formative tendency or master motive at work in the universe reads more like poetry or religion than science. A hard-headed biologist is likely to shy away from any such suggestion implying direction in evolution. But for Rogers it is a fact of observation, apparent first in the baby's efforts to master the world. Out of this striving emerges one particular set of experiences, which are always present: these are the baby's experiences of relationships with others, which eventually coalesce to form the self; and the child can say 'I'. Later the adult can say 'I don't see myself as a teacher' or 'I only really feel myself when I'm with my family'.

But though Rogers may be giving an account of the self or Me of common sense, he is failing to explain the I. The I of 'I don't see myself as a teacher' cannot be both my*self* that is seen and whatever does the seeing; it cannot be both object and subject. The I does the seeing . . . and the thinking and deciding and feeling. I apply for a place at teacher training college; it is not my self that does. I may decide to apply because I see my*self* as a teacher rather than as a doctor, but the self cannot be both what sees and what is seen, feels and is felt. Rogers' self is not the I that does the seeing and feeling, applies for teacher training or decides not to, feels the pain in the leg, is depressed, and is aware of the self. Rogers fails to account for this I.

Rogers regards experience as central but he fails to explain what the I is that does the experiencing. He takes care to avoid any suggestion of a little man inside twitching the strings, and he says that the whole human organism feels, acts, reacts, decides, experiences, though it does so with reference to the self. But simply to say the whole organism feels, acts and decides is to evade an issue that is central to any account of personality and crucial to one that emphasizes experience. What is this 'thing' which experiences and which common sense calls the 'I'?

As I approach the traffic lights they turn yellow and I have to decide what to do. I am going to the dentist tomorrow and I feel anxious. Rogers fails to account not only for the I which decides and fears, but also for this I which is aware of my trying to decide whether to stop or to jump the lights, and which is conscious of being anxious about tomorrow's visit to the dentist. No other animal has this sort of self-consciousness – or certainly not to the same degree. Rogers' talk of self might lead one to suppose that he has solved something about mind, but he has explained nothing, neither what it is nor how it originates.

With regard to the question of free will, Rogers' experience over many years was that real change did occur in therapy. A woman sits, anxious and depressed; since childhood she has felt only anger for the father who bullied and crushed her. Gradually in therapy she chooses to let go her anger and to forgive her father, even to love him. She did not change – and people do not change – because unconscious forces become conscious. Nor did she change because she has been reshaped by new patterns of reward and punishment. People change in therapy because they come to see them*selves* and their situation differently, and this they choose to do. Therapy, and life, is about free human beings struggling to become more free. In the love–hate relationship that a husband and wife have in their marriage, there is choice as to whether the love or the hate will prevail in the end. Personal experience is important and affects what we do, but it does not imprison us.

How we react to our experience is something we ourselves choose and decide, and Janet can react to Michael's departure in a number of ways. She can choose to keep up the façade and continue the pretence of being always cheerful, or she can admit she is depressed. The love with strings attached that she received as a child makes it difficult for her to be honest and to know what she really feels, and may mean that she needs therapy. But with the help of therapy, or possibly without it, Janet is free either to let Michael go and accept the pain or to decide to commit herself to the relationship and ask him to return.

But having gone this far and seemingly committed himself to human freedom, Rogers does an about-turn. In *Freedom to Learn for the 80's* he asserts: 'Yet as we enter this field of psychotherapy with objective research methods, we are, like any other scientist, committed to a complete determinism'. Science works on the assumption of cause and effect – if I am ill and go to the surgery the doctor tries to find a cause. When the TV set stops working and the engineer cannot find out why, he does not assume that there is a poltergeist in the set but goes on looking for a material cause. It is becoming clear from science, says Rogers, that human beings are complex machines and not free.

It is surprising that Rogers should feel obliged to give up his belief that human beings are free on the say-so of science. If this science is right, then the great plays of Shakespeare are based on an illusion . Hamlet had no choice about 'To be or not to be', and Macbeth could not help murdering King Duncan or Brutus killing Caesar, even though they agonized over the 'decision'. It is particularly odd that Rogers should feel obliged on the say-so of science to abandon his belief in human freedom, since his belief is based on his own experience, and he has always stressed the validity of experience.

As a result he ends up holding two opposing views. On the one hand there exists science which, according to Rogers, says that human actions are caused and determined, like everything else. On the other hand there is psychotherapy in which, in Rogers' experience, people change . . . and they change because they choose to change, and they can choose to change because they are free. Rogers concedes that there is no satisfactory reconciliation of these two opposing positions and that we have to live with the paradox. At the same time, he does attempt a reconciliation of the sort usually called soft determinism.

Soft determinism says that all behaviour is caused, but some behaviour is caused and free. Soft determinists argue that there is no contradiction between determinism and the belief that human beings are sometimes free. Soft determinists hold that, though what humans do is completely caused, they remain responsible for what they do. Freud, regarded by some as a hard determinist and by others as believing that human beings have a modest degree of freedom, has also been seen as a soft determinist. How behaviour can be both determined and free is the question that soft determinists have to answer.

My behaviour is caused by a variety of desires, and among them are rational desires about how I want to behave – this is how the argument for soft determinism usually begins. I want to dominate rather than love, or act kindly rather than cruelly, or get up rather than stay in bed. These desires influence and cause my actions. I do something because I want to – which means my action is caused and determined. But I do it only because I want to – which means that my action is free.

What is it that makes these free but caused actions of soft determinism different from those which everyone would agree are determined, such as those of a man who is drugged or drunk or threatened or obsessionally driven by a neurosis? It is not that in these other situations there are causes but that there are no causes in the soft determinist situation – there are causes present in both kinds of situation. What is different is the kind of causes present. In the first situation, the soft determinist argues, there is a unique kind of cause present, a motive or want or desire, that leaves the individual free.

Rogers' own soft determinism begins by pointing out that what is characteristic of neurotic and (to use his term) incongruent people is their defensiveness. Their defensiveness forces them to act in a way in which they would prefer not to. They hate when they would rather love, hold back when they would rather give themselves, stay in a job they dislike rather than risk something new. But healthy, fully functioning people are not on the defensive. 'The fully functioning person, on the other hand, not only experiences, but utilizes, the most absolute freedom when he spontaneously, freely, and voluntarily chooses and wills that which is absolutely determined,' says Rogers in *Freedom to Learn*. Fully functioning people are open to experience and behave in a certain way – the way they have to – because it is the most satisfying. Like the cowboy hero who does what he does because 'a man's gotta do what a man's gotta do', fully functioning people *choose* to act the way they *have to* because it is the most fulfilling. Free individuals choose to act as cause and effect determines they must, but they are free in what they do and, like a plant growing towards the light, they have no choice! In Rogers' own words, 'The free person moves out voluntarily, freely, responsibly, to play her significant part in a world whose determined events move through her and through her spontaneous choice and will' (*Freedom to Learn*). This is the kingdom of soft determinism.

Hard determinists and libertarians, who believe that human beings are free, are able to agree on one thing: the absurdity of the soft determinist position. They agree that our behaviour cannot be both free and caused at the same time. Though Rogers is unlikely to agree with William James's assertion that soft determinism is 'a quagmire of evasion', he concedes that the paradox remains.

Rogers, taking a more optimistic view of human beings than Freud, has made a considerable contribution to the development of what is called humanistic psychology. With his theory and his subsequent research, he gave scientific respectability to the common-sense notion of the self. He made us aware how important it is to value our*selves* and – for this to be possible – how crucial it is to have been loved without strings. He made respectable in modern psychology the idea that individuals can take charge of their lives, and this led to his creating a non-directive therapy. In this new approach the initiative could be left to the persons in therapy (no longer called clients or patients) since they knew what was best for them. Rogers believed this new psychotherapy helped people in months rather than years. He affirmed that in therapy and in life we are able to develop into good and psychologically healthy people, given the right conditions. We can all live fulfilled, satisfying lives if we adopt the right attitude. He made us aware that what really matters is not the 'real' world but our attitude towards it and to our self, and how we choose to see them.

Economic progress in the West has raised expectations about the material conditions of life. Parallel with this, Rogers and similarly minded humanist psychologists have raised expectations about the personal life and particularly about human relationships. The influence of Rogers and others has led us to regard fulfilment in our lives and the realizing of our human potential as right and good. They have influenced us so that we now place fulfilment and satisfaction in our lives above any Victorian notion of duty – though we shall see that for Rogers there is really no moral conflict.

Does Rogers believe that human beings have a moral dimension distinguishing right from wrong? Yes, he does. But it is unusual, not at all like Pinocchio's Jiminy Cricket; the latter attaches himself to the puppet as a vocal external conscience. Nor is it a voice like Freud's superego, external to begin with but ending up inside. Quite simply, human beings know what is best for them.

In a well-known experiment, young children were given a variety of unflavoured foods to choose from for their meals. Over a period the diet they selected for themselves was very satisfactory. A child eating an excessive amount of starch began to balance this after a while by eating more protein. A child concentrating for a time on foods lacking a certain vitamin eventually ate foods which had that particular vitamin. Referring to this experiment, Rogers speaks of a 'physiological wisdom' of the body guiding the children's choices. There is also a wisdom of the whole human, a 'valuing process' that knows what is morally good for it. This valuing process is innate and resembles the old-fashioned conscience of religion. The conscience of traditional religion is God's voice within, distinguishing between right and wrong in the interests of the soul's salvation. Rogers' valuing process distinguishes between right and wrong in the interests of living a fulfilled human life and achieving our true potential.

There is nothing odd in such a suggestion. All a daffodil bulb needs in order to grow to its right size and shape and colour is nourishment, moisture, light. It is the very nature of the bulb to develop into a healthy, lovely daffodil, and it will always do so, given the right conditions. Human beings are no different, and if they are given the right condition, which is love without strings, a moral dimension will inevitably emerge. The values which this moral dimension asserts, its 'right' and 'good', are those that favour human fulfilment and lead to the fully functioning person.

Rogers had observed in therapy that when human beings listen to this voice something interesting happens. Whatever their culture or background the direction of their development is the same. Like the children opting for the same balanced diet, in therapy people tend eventually to opt for similar values. Morality is no illusion, and we are moral beings. Right and wrong, good and bad do exist and are much the same everywhere. The idea that moral values are relative is nonsense. No one emerges from therapy preferring hate to love, valuing contempt above compassion, regarding it right to exploit others, or good to abuse children and neglect ageing parents.

Rogers' view resembles that of many religions and of common sense. There is a moral dimension in human beings that is part of their nature, and the difference between right and wrong, good and bad, is real. The difference between Martin Luther King and Stalin, between Mother Teresa and Hitler is no fiction, nor is it the difference between a well-trained and a badly trained dog. It is the difference between psychological health and psychological sickness because, for Rogers, this is the difference between right and wrong. He provides no scientific explanation of this moral dimension, such as a possible herd instinct. But then neither does religion or common sense, other than to say it is part of human nature.

Skinner's humans exist in a bird-cage. Good is what we do that is rewarding to others, which is why they feed us.

Bad is what we do which hurts others, which is why they punish us. Freud's men and women are not actually bad – the word has no meaning – but they are certainly dangerous. They emerge from the animal jungle scored through with something like Original Sin. Rogers' flower people come from before any Fall, with an original good intact, seeking only peace, love and understanding.

But a Fall does eventually occur, and it happens when parents attach conditions to their love. If we had been loved unconditionally as children and could now trust our feelings and experience, we would certainly be good. If parents had loved us without strings we would be living fulfilled lives and becoming truly human. This is what happens in therapy when humans feel free, unthreatened and safe. A person may have murderous feelings, contempt, perverse sexual impulses to begin with; but when change happens, triggered off by the empathy and unconditional love of the therapist, it moves in one direction. Hate dissipates to reveal the love beneath, contempt becomes compassion, a sadistic or odd sexuality turns into one based on relationship. Human nature exists, is moral, and is good.

The love and understanding of flower-power is not just a strand in our nature; loving and understanding is what we strive to become because this is our true nature. Irritated by Jiminy Cricket, Pinocchio eventually crushes him. But the voice of Jiminy is not easily silenced and he returns as a ghost to haunt Pinocchio. Similarly, the voice of our true nature is not stilled by childhoods in which we were not loved for what we were. In the freedom of therapy or the right conditions in life, humans struggle to achieve their true being. In Freud's view, if we were allowed to follow our true nature, it would be back to the jungle for all of us as unrepressed sexuality and aggression broke loose. Skinner believed our nature to be neutral, and we become what reward and punishment make us. But for Rogers the result of achieving our true nature, in therapy or in life, would be the same as for Pinocchio: we cease to be puppets and become fully human.

What is this human we would be if love with strings attached had not distorted our true nature? What is this human person we can become again if the empathy and unconditional love (of therapy or friendship or marriage) enable us to achieve our true self? It is good; it is loving, trustworthy, constructive, realistic and rational. We can – and do – go badly wrong, but our deepest tendencies are always moving in the direction of the true interests of ourselves and others. This is what Rogers found in therapy.

In his paintings of Tahiti, Gauguin evoked a paradise of innocent and good people. Tahiti is a part of the Polynesia described by Margaret Mead in her best-selling anthropological study, *Coming of Age in Samoa*. She describes a tropical island where life began with a relaxed childhood, free from stress and pressure, with little or no punishment. What followed was an adolescence that was free from the conflict and strain found among teenagers in the West. In Samoa, according to Mead, adolescence was fun, a time of easy, guilt-free and casual sexual relations. Aggression, violence and competition were rare among Samoan adults; they were co-operative and free of the obsession with rank and prestige that is found in other societies. The sunshine, mild climate, lush vegetation, abundance of food but, above all, the culture and the way children were brought up made this an island paradise where the good life was possible.

In a recent book, *Margaret Mead and Samoa*, Derek Freeman presents evidence which suggests that she got it wrong. At the time of her study, Samoa was no nearer to achieving the good life than any other society. Childhood there was not particularly happy or relaxed, and children were often punished, sometimes even beaten quite harshly. Adolescence was not the fun-time Mead described, nor was it made easy by a tolerance of sexual permissiveness. The adult Samoans prized virginity before marriage; and adolescence was a period of considerable stress and conflict. Samoan society was intensely competitive, with both men and women obsessed with prestige and social status. The levels of rape, murder and suicide were high. Freeman's account of Samoa and his criticism of Mead have been criticized in their turn, but it seems that he was sufficiently right to confirm what common sense had already suspected: there are no known paradises on this earth. If a paradise garden peopled by only good men and women exists somewhere, it has yet to be found.

There is great goodness in human beings, according to Rogers. The potential for goodness is basic, and bad is the result only of distortion. We are born like Rousseau's noble savage, inclined only to good, and are twisted from our true nature by love with strings attached. The question that has to be asked is whether Rogers accounts adequately for human violence, aggression, cruelty.

Common observation suggests that if there are many good Rogerian people about and possibly a few saints, there are some nasty sinners around too; and most of us are a mixture of good and bad. Human beings are neither angel nor beast: born into a world where good and bad exist, however, we are immediately implicated. There is already a serpent in paradise. We are all affected by our childhood, by our circumstances and our biology, but what we are is also the result of free choice.

The Bible which begins with the story of the Fall in the Garden swiftly follows with an account of a brother's murder; and for the first time there exists an animal that, deliberately and often, kills its own kind. Like Cain and Abel, we enter a world where good and bad already exist and are immediately caught up in their interplay, but the choice remains ours. This is the common-sense view. But with the idea of choice we return to that freedom which Rogers' experience tells him exists, but which in the name of science he cannot quite accept.

Chapter Five

LONELY LIBERALS:
Erich Fromm's neo-Freudianism

Homelessness has become a world fate.
>   Heidegger: 'Letter on Humanism'

In Dostoevsky's *The Brothers Karamazov*, Christ returns to medieval Spain. He is recognized and excited crowds gather and follow, until the Grand Inquisitor of Seville has Him arrested and taken to the dungeons of the inquisition. Later the Grand Inquisitor interrogates Christ and reproaches Him for starting a religion of freedom – human beings do not wish to be free, he explains. So unbearable do they find being free that the Church has been forced to become authoritarian and relieve them of freedom by insisting on obedience. The inquisition is for those who disobey; but for those who do obey, the Church guarantees salvation. This arrangement is what people want, the Grand Inquisitor explains to Christ: 'There is nothing a man is more anxious to do than find someone to whom he can hand over as quickly as possible the gift of freedom with which the poor creature was born.'

Like Dostoevsky, Fromm was troubled by the flight from freedom into authoritarian beliefs and totalitarian regimes. Why in the twentieth century had people swarmed to join Nazism and Fascism and other sick '-isms'? Why did modern society produce organization men and women, happy to hand over their personal responsibility to commercial corporations, political parties and state governments? In answering these questions, Fromm was investigating the nature of human beings, and his answer begins in our evolutionary past.

In the Bible story, Adam and Eve are one with God and nature. There is no work, no struggle to exist, no pain, discord or loneliness, only peace and harmony. There is no freedom either; it is the peace and harmony of the womb. Adam and Eve must do what God tells them and not eat the fruit of the forbidden tree. All this ended when in one act of rebellion they ate the apple and God banished them from paradise. The womb-like existence of the paradise garden was over and humans became separate from the rest of nature. They were on their own now, alone in the world, with no heavenly father to guide them and talk to them in the cool of the evening. Fromm sees the Adam and Eve story as myth – human beings are a consequence of evolution. But the myth tells us that, as evolution progressed, humans became separate from the rest of nature. The myth ends with Adam and Eve alone, without God, outside paradise and about to begin their journey through the world. There is no going back because God posted angels with flaming swords at the gates. For Fromm, what started as biological evolution became also a psychological separation as humans emerged and developed into separate beings. They were part of nature still but apart from nature, each a freak of the material universe, and free.

In Fromm's account, what happened next was the creation of primitive creeds and religious beliefs to enable these separate humans to feel at home in the world they were part of but apart from. In Europe, in very recent times, the Catholic Church filled this role and provided such security. Dostoevsky's legend of the Grand Inquisitor parodied the more extreme forms this took. But the Catholic Church with its dogmas and sacraments spelled out to believers that God was in His heaven and that this world could be tolerated because all would be well in the next. Fromm saw that the Church, as mediator between God and humanity, guaranteeing salvation and promising that ultimately everything was well, limited human freedom. The Reformation put an end to this.

By the time that the wars of the German Protestant princes were over, the power of the Roman Catholic Church was broken. In a production of John Osborne's *Luther*, the founder of Protestantism stands at the edge of a battlefield, appalled by what he has done. The Catholic Church no longer exists to embrace Europe in a community of belief, dogma and practice. Now there is nothing to provide men and women with the security of a God-ordained order, to give value and meaning to human life. 'You are your own priest now,' said Luther. Fromm believed that at this moment the men and women of Europe became free . . . but also alone in a meaningless universe. Separation – both physical and psychological separation from nature, and psychological separation from dogma and authority – makes people free. But separation makes people alone, and potentially insignificant and lonely.

This is the terrible reality from which the Grand Inquisitor had spared the Catholics of medieval Spain but from which, in Fromm's view, modern men and women cannot be spared. Without dogmas imposed by church and society we are free individuals, and this we welcome. But as free individuals, without religion and a community of believers, we are alone and insecure, our lives without meaning.

There is a way to rid ourselves of this loneliness and lack of meaning: give up the freedom that causes them. Keep a hold on nurse, 'For fear of finding something worse.' Fromm saw why men and women embraced authoritarian organizations and totalitarian regimes: it was to escape freedom.

Subjects in a psychological experiment who thought something unpleasant was about to be done to them could choose to wait with others or sit alone; they chose to wait with others. But modern men and women do not find waiting with others sufficiently reassuring. They must bind themselves to others in mass movements and totalitarian ideologies. Only in this way do they escape the freedom they find so unbearable. But before examining further the plight of modern men and women, we need to look at Fromm's general account of human personality and society. This is best done by relating him to three other thinkers: Freud, Marx and Weber.

Fromm agrees with Freud that what goes on in the family shapes the child's personality. A child stuck at the early breast-feeding stage grows up an oral passive adult, clinging, lacking initiative, dependent. For Freud the biology of breast-feeding shapes personality. Fromm believes it is not biology and instinct but relationships which shape personality.

If a child grows up clinging, lacking initiative or dependent, it is because of the relationships the child experienced within the family. Mother was domineering, refused to allow any initiative, checked any assertiveness, insisted that the child was submissive. And Mother's manner of breast-feeding – because of her personality – was also smothering and oppressive. Freud has grasped the relationship between Mother's breast-feeding and the child's personality but has not grasped what caused what. What really caused the child to grow up a passive oral adult was Mother's personality, not her breast-feeding. Mother's domineering personality emerged in many ways, one of which was in the way she breast-fed. For Freud the satisfaction of instincts is all-important and largely decides personality. For Fromm human relationships, not biology, are all-important.

A child gets stuck at the late anal stage. The adult that emerges is characterized by the unholy trinity of obstinacy, tidiness, meanness, plus a tendency to constipation. What causes fixation at the anal stage, says Freud, is the bodily instinct of elimination that toilet training has to control. It is the other way around, says Fromm. Obstinacy, tidiness, meanness are ways of relating to the world and to other people, and these we learn from our parents. In a particular family a child learns to be stubborn, to keep everything in its right place, not to trust others, never to relax and let go. Mother may teach a child this in many ways, but one way will be in her manner of toilet training. The personality that results is the controlling late anal character which tends to constipation. For Fromm, the personality of parents operating through relationships with the child, and emerging – among other ways – in the way they toilet train, shapes the child's personality.

At the phallic stage, according to Freud, it is biology again, now that of sex, that determines personality. If an excessively strong sexual bond develops between boy and mother, problems of personal relations will arise when the boy grows up, as they did with Hamlet. It is the other way around, says Fromm. The oedipus conflict is not caused by sexual instinct getting fixated; it is caused by poor personal relations.

Fromm believes that in patriarchal societies fathers represent society's repressive authority. When a boy grows up and wants to become free and independent, the omnipotent father tries, God-like, to crush him. The Adam-and-Eve myth is as much about the growth of personality as about the evolution of the human species. An oedipus complex results when a boy fails to sort out his relationship with his father by standing up to him. Freud was right when he said the oedipus conflict was at the root of every neurosis, but it has little to do with sex, instinct and biology. The key problem for every individual is that of human relations, and these start in the family. It is in this sense, Fromm says, that the family shapes personality.

But the sorts of human relations shaping Hamlet's personality were not unique to the royal family at Elsinore. The family does not exist in a vacuum but in a wider society. Hamlet's struggle with his new stepfather is one example of the fight for dominance found among males in all patriarchal cultures. In such societies, human relations among males centre round power. Women are incidental – they are part of the spoils. Succeed in toppling Father, and Mother is yours. *Hamlet*, like the Adam-and-Eve myth and the Oedipus story, is about the rebellion of sons against fathers among upper-class families in patriarchal societies. Hamlet's mother merely goes with the throne. Fromm argues that what happens in any family is caused by the wider society and by the family's position in that society, particularly its class. His reading of Marx had convinced him that both class and society influence and shape the family and the relationships within it.

'The rich really are different,' Scott Fitzgerald said to Ernest Hemingway. 'No, Scott,' Hemingway replied, 'they just have more money.' Hemingway is thought to have got the better of the exchange; but Karl Marx, aware how economic factors shape human lives, would have agreed with Scott Fitzgerald. Economic factors form personality. Having more (or less) money does make a difference, as Fitzgerald's Great Gatsby was aware. '"She's got an indiscreet voice," I remarked. "It's full of –" I hesitated. "Her voice is full of money," he said suddenly.'

The late anal personality which Fromm regards as typically lower-middle-class is the result of its position in capitalist society. Clerks, toolmakers, grocers live the way they do because of their income. They cannot afford to take risks because their incomes are low. If they got into serious debt they would have difficulty getting out of it, so they rarely overdraw at the bank. When they do, they are not at peace until they have cleared the overdraft. But their incomes are reliable, and they play to their strength by eking out their steady income carefully, saving when they can, taking three buses rather than a taxi. Carefulness with money is what the lower-middle class need in order to survive in a capitalist society. They lead orderly lives, take no risks and – apart from a 'flutter' on the Grand National – never gamble. They live in tidy houses, save and – if redundancy threatens – save even harder. Redundant manual workers typically 'blow' redundancy money on a good holiday.

But the lower-middle class do not feel trapped. The influence of income and class on family and its members goes even deeper. What family upbringing does, in Fromm's view, is so shape us that we end up *wanting* to act the way we *have* to. So effective is the family in shaping personality that the lower-middle class have no desire to be any different. Quite the reverse – they wax morally indignant when others act differently from themselves, condemning both the wastefulness of the rich and working-class fecklessness. But the rich and the working class also have the personalities they have because of family income and class. Daisy in *The Great Gatsby* cannot help her voice being full of money any more than a working man can help spending his redundancy money on a holiday rather than investing it.

For Freud the structure of personality is universal and exists for all time. Personality is based on biology, and biology never changes – except over hundreds of thousands of years. But according to Fromm, we are shaped by personal relationships within our family and these are shaped by the wider society.

These vary from class to class, and change when society changes.

If Fromm's account of the lower-middle class now reads a little out of date, it makes this very point. As society and the economic situation change, what goes on in a family changes. The lower-middle class is more assertive nowadays than when Fromm originally wrote. It throws its money around more, occasionally enters the betting shop, goes abroad on package holidays. It does this because of economic changes. Lower-middle-class jobs are no longer secure and guaranteed for life. With rapid technological change, being careful and clinging to the old ways is no longer a sound strategy for survival. So shopkeepers and clerks and skilled workers now teach their children to be more flexible, to adapt to new ways, to take risks, to become computer operators and programmers. The economic forces affecting the lower-middle class have changed, so the personality of the lower-middle class has changed.

Whatever the class, whether lower or upper-middle, lower- or upper-working, aristocracy or *nouveau riche*, a social character arises common to a particular class because of its economic situation. This is Fromm's Marxism. He has used Freud to give Marxism a psychology, and used Marxism to give personality a social and economic context. Scott Fitzgerald was right – 'The rich really are different', and so is every other class.

A third influence on Fromm was the German sociologist, Max Weber, who argued – it seems common sense enough – that ideas influence events. Marx believed that economic forces and methods of production decide what goes on in society and shape its ideas, beliefs, values. For Weber the reverse was also true: people's ideas, beliefs and values affect what happens in society. The destruction of the power of the Catholic Church may have been completed by the armies of the German princes, but it began with the ideas of Protestantism. The ideas led to the armies.

Fromm agreed with Weber that ideas, beliefs and values even shape the economic structures and forces which Marx regarded as all-important. Common sense confirms this: we observe that when governments are committed to certain economic theories, such as monetarism or socialism, the economic repercussions are considerable. Human ideas have power, and the ideas of Protestantism which broke the structure of the Catholic Church went on to cause an economic system called capitalism. For Fromm this historical development had repercussions for personality.

When the Catholic Church with its community and comforting assurances no longer had its old influence, what were people to do? Calvin and Protestantism came up with an answer: they must work, because to work is to do the will of God. You are alone before God, said Protestantism, but if your work succeeds, this is your guarantee of God's approval which the Catholic Church is no longer in a position to give.

But if one worked and succeeded, what should be done with the profits? Wine, women and song were out, since they conflicted with other Protestant values. One might resort to the medieval idea of charity and give to the poor, but this no longer seemed a good idea. If success and wealth were a sign of God's approval, failure and poverty were as sure a sign of His disfavour. It could not be right to give one's God-approved profits to the undeserving poor whose very poverty was evidence of moral bankruptcy. The alternative was to make use of profits to finance new work, buy more land, invest in one's own and other people's developments.

Fromm saw that ideas, beliefs and values, acting through personality, cause economic development. These particular beliefs and values, the ethic of early Protestantism, brought about capitalism. But Fromm also saw, with Marx, that economic developments by shaping personality give rise to certain ideas, values and beliefs. The steam engine is a product both of human individuals and of the economic society that formed the individuals who invented it. And so a cycle is created. The economic basis of society forms human social personality, and personality shapes ideas, values, beliefs. In turn these ideas, values and beliefs acting through personality determine the economic basis of society – and the cycle is complete. On this cycle Fromm saw everything in history developing. On this cycle capitalism, industrial society and eventually the twentieth century emerged. From Fromm's general account of personality and society, we return to his account of how they are now.

In John Osborne's play, *Breakfast in Amsterdam*, three couples talk incessantly about the boss they have left in London. They joke about him, criticize him and complain bitterly about him. But when they awake the following morning to the news of his death, they feel no relief or liberation, only loneliness and fear; and this in part is how Fromm sees our situation now. We have been separated from nature and from other people by evolution and our emergence as individuals. Until recently, in the West the Catholic Church acted as an intermediary between human beings and a benevolent God. While Protestantism flourished, humans still had a meaningful place in the universe, but one depending on a personal relationship with God. In the nineteenth century with industrialization and the growth of capitalism, human beings came to have no value other than an economic one, and the universe turned into a machine. God had no place in such a landscape; and at the close of the century Nietzsche announced His death. God's death, with the advance of the unfree machine and the cost-obsessed balance sheet, left people alienated and lonely, their lives without meaning or significance. Human personality cannot be understood outside its social and economic situation, and this was how Fromm regarded the situation of twentieth-century men and women.

Fromm saw the central problem for human personality in modern times was, how to live in a Godless, meaningless universe. For many the answer lay in a flight to authoritarian beliefs and totalitarian regimes. For Fromm the true solution is to be found in using our freedom. But in Fromm's account so far there is an emphasis on what causes and shapes personality and behaviour, so where – according to Fromm – is human freedom to be found?

Faust sells his soul to the devil and later, when death approaches, cannot find it in himself to repent. Fromm believes it is possible for people to become like Faust and to be determined in what they do because they have forfeited their freedom. At the end of their lives, Hitler and Stalin are unlikely to have found it in themselves to grieve for the suffering they caused. At the other extreme, Fromm believes there are a fortunate few who, because of lives of right choices and actions, can eventually opt only for what is right and good. They have arrived at a blessed state in which they are no longer free to choose evil and to do wrong. Their personalities are fixed by the good they have done. We cannot imagine an elderly St Francis suddenly going to the bad. At both extremes, as a result of a lifetime of bad or good, an individual will no longer be free. Some like Faust can do only bad, while others, like St Francis, can do only good.

How did these people ever get into their sorry or their blessed state? With the former, it was like Hogarth's *Rake's Progress*, just one damn and damning thing after another. The rake's first bad act was a free choice; once done, it made the second easier, and the second made the third easier, and the third made the fourth easier still. At these early stages the rake remained free and able to choose. But with every bad act he became less free, until eventually he arrived at the nth bad act. By this time he had declined and fallen to such an extent that he could no longer help himself. He was no longer free because his personality had lost any capacity to choose good. By a similar but happier progress, our saint-in-the-making does one good turn after another, with them getting easier every time. Eventually he or she is no longer free, having lost any inclination or capacity to choose to do wrong.

At these extremes Fromm believes that human behaviour is caused and determined. After many years of drinking I am no longer free to stop – they say no alcoholic is ever really cured. The forces working on my personality have become so strong that they determine what I do: as an oral passive adult to start with, because of my childhood, and with my adult habits of drinking so rooted, I am not free to change now.

But most of us are not yet alcoholics, compulsive smokers or gamblers, saints, irredeemably bad, irreproachably good or incurably kind. It is only at the end of a long chain of acts that such determinism operates. Earlier along the line I am free, to drink or not to, to act well, to act badly, and this is the position most of us are in. In Fromm's view, most of us remain such a fine balance of contradictory inclinations that we are usually in a position to choose.

But freedom is never absolute, and it is always restricted by the alternatives available. Bored and irritated at a meeting I am obliged to attend, I may be free to choose between being aggressive and saying nothing; but I may not have it in me to get up quietly and leave the meeting early. Fromm believes that human beings are free when their inclinations are balanced, but even then they can choose only from the options available. But free they usually are, within limits, to change themselves, their character, their ideas, and free to change the family relationships and economic forces that shaped them in the first place.

Human freedom turns on a key decision that everyone is faced with. Either I accept, even welcome, that I am free ... after a long depression William James wrote in his diary: 'My first act of free-will shall be to believe in free-will.' Or I can choose to escape from that freedom by surrendering myself and my freedom to a person, ideology or organization – according to the Grand Inquisitor, this is what people really want. We can either embrace our freedom or fly from it. Fromm has described the choice as between humanistic and authoritarian attitudes, between the productive and non-productive character, between being and having. Fromm believed that our personalities are shaped by economic forces, family relationships, ideas and values, but also by our choices, because choice certainly exists. The choice enters into and affects all areas of life: personal relations, sexual relations, politics, religion, being a parent, being an employer. It is a choice which we have no alternative but to make one way or the other and to go on making. For Fromm, accepting and welcoming that freedom is the only true solution to the human situation. But, as we shall see later, Fromm's account of human freedom is merely a description, not an explanation.

It is the use that we make of our freedom, together with economic forces, family relationships, and ideas, beliefs and values, that forms our personality. Fromm divides personality into five main types: the productive character who embraces freedom, and the receptive, exploitative, hoarding and marketing characters who choose not to be free.

Receptive characters feel nothing worthwhile inside them.

Everything good comes from outside, and this they passively accept, whether it be help, opinions – they have so few of their own – or the love they crave. Receptive characters are submissive, they lean heavily on others and, if religious, they believe that 'God will provide'. On the positive side they are devoted, modest, often optimistic, they enjoy their food and drink, resembling Freud's early oral suckers. They avoid the demands of freedom by being dependent, inoffensive and lovable, so that others will do everything for them.

A key element in their psychology is what Fromm calls masochism. This masochism emerges as a search for a magic helper. I rid myself of my freedom by submitting to someone or something more powerful. I marry and do as my husband tells me. I join the Party, put on a uniform, and follow the Party line. By submitting I cease to have a separate self which would feel lonely and insignificant. The Me that remains takes on the power of what I submit to, be it husband or Party or organization. I join a multi-national corporation, become an organization man, and what is good for the company is good for me and good for everyone else. The need for moral choices is gone. When I lay down my freedom at someone else's feet – my husband's, the Party's, the company's – and identify with them, I become something, somebody, and my loneliness and insignificance disappear. Receptive characters show excessive devotion, duty and 'love' because of the inadequacy they feel, which their masochism is a way of escaping. Their dependency makes it hard for them to say 'No' – they will love anyone who loves them. Depending so much on others they have no opinion until they know what the *Daily Express* or the *Guardian*, the Pope or the Kremlin, has to say. For the receptive character, masochism achieves what the Grand Inquisitor was after for believers: getting rid of unbearable freedom by submitting. Receptive characters idealize those above them. They do not have ordinary mothers and fathers but parents who are saints, and Mother's Day and Father's Day on which to venerate them.

People take the shape that enables them to survive in their particular society with its specific ideas, values, beliefs and economic system. Receptive characters are made by societies in which one group dominates another. Feudal serfs would tend to be receptive characters; slaves and domestic servants might become so. The subordinate group, powerless and with no control over its own destiny, has no alternative but to look to the dominating group to provide. Receptive characters are also formed in hierarchical societies in which a paternal but powerful aristocracy treats the 'lower orders' with kindly condescension, so long as they touch their forelocks and conform. Modern consumer society makes receptive characters of us all as we gaze passively at the adverts to see what goodies on the outside will fill up our emptiness inside.

Exploitative characters are different. They also feel that good things are only on the outside, but they believe that they are there to be got by cunning or force. Whatever it is that the exploitative character takes from others, whether objects, ideas or pleasure, these seem all the better for having been acquired in this way, just as St Augustine's apple tasted sweeter for having been stolen. On the positive side exploitative characters are active, self-confident and show initiative. They avoid the loneliness and insignificance that freedom brings, by outsmarting others, attacking them, getting one up on them, and as a result feeling powerful and superior.

Exploitative characters are related to Freud's oral sadistic personality, and sadism is central to their psychology. In Camus' novel *The Outsider*, Salamano constantly curses and kicks and generally bullies his dog, and seems to loathe the animal. But when the dog disappears Salamano is bereft. Dominating and damaging the animal had made Salamano feel strong and kept his loneliness at bay. An exploitative mother claims that she dominates her children because she loves them, but it is the other way around. She 'loves' her children because she can dominate them, and she is prepared to give them everything except the one thing they want – their freedom. Holding on to them and dominating them she feels important and real – though in this way she forfeits any possibility either for herself or for them to be free. But the last thing she wants is freedom, hers or theirs.

Like Salamano and his dog and the mother with her children, exploitative characters need the object of their sadism. A wife-battering husband says he wants to be rid of his wife and keeps telling her to go. When she does eventually walk out, he is soon round at the local women's refuge begging her to return. The last thing he wants is to be without her, as he feels real only when he is bullying.

This sadistic flight from freedom illustrates Fromm's neat reversal of Freud's notion of sadism. Freud would say that the man hits his wife for the sexual pleasure he derives from perverted instinct. For Fromm, sadism is about wanting to dominate people and what has been perverted is human relations. Sadism may occasionally express itself sexually; but what comes first is not biology and instinct but psychology and human relations. Stalin's delight in ordering the torture or execution of the friend or wife of an official was non-sexual sadism; Stalin would leave the official himself untouched, because once he killed the official his pleasure would be gone. The sadism of exploitative characters fuses them with the object of their sadism, and this stops them feeling separate and lonely. Sadism, with its contempt for the scum below, is the obverse of masochism's reverence for those above. Both combine in the authoritarian personality, like that of the Nazi who kicks the non-Aryans beneath him and who bows and scrapes before his Führer.

What kinds of societies are most likely to shape humans into exploitative characters? They are societies in which economic and moral controls are few, the laws of the jungle hold, and where rewards for success are high. A situation of *laissez-faire* economics, the early stages of capitalism, a free-booting colonialism, are fine moulders of such characters. In Western society, the rapacious imperialism of the late nineteenth century was a time which favoured exploitative individuals like Cecil Rhodes. At certain times, says Fromm, capitalism needs people of initiative, ruthlessness, ambition and with a desire to dominate, to go out and grab; so society, working through the family, shapes men (and women) to become like this.

In contrast to receptive and exploitative characters, who regard only what is outside as worth while, Fromm sees hoarding characters as valuing only what is inside and their own.

Hoarding characters may collect first editions – but not because they like books; possession satisfies. Hoarders, feeling that things wear out and do not get replenished, hold on to and control what they have. On the positive side they are careful, orderly, tenacious, obsessively hard-working. They are cold fish because they cope with their own feelings of insignificance and loneliness by insulating themselves against other people. They hold back, in order to keep powerlessness, loneliness and change at bay, by hanging on tight to what they have: money, property, ideas, stamps, faeces. Fromm's hoarding character is close cousin to Freud's late anal personality.

A key trait of a hoarder is destructiveness. The hoarder enjoys destroying whatever is living, like the general who loved nothing better than the smell of napalm in the morning. Control is what the hoarding personality is after, and destruction is a particularly nasty way of achieving it. Having destroyed the enemy I am alone, but I am in splendid isolation and master of all I survey. Such destructiveness is an escape from loneliness and insignificance; the mugger or the Nazi staring down at his victim feels powerful and real. Fromm sees a society in which one group or class dominates another as a good breeding-ground for destructively inclined hoarders.

Industrial cultures shape more normal hoarders, the dutiful employees such societies need – or have needed until now. Industrial capitalism has depended upon thrifty characters, who are careful with money and who arrive regularly for work and on time. Such people emerged particularly from the lower-middle class; seeing themselves as having an investment in things as they are, they held on to what they had and supported the status quo. Living on low salaries, needing to be careful with money, buying a house and reluctant to get into debt, the lower-middle class provided a workforce which acted as a buffer between the managerial middle class and the more aggressive proletariat. They were also a useful source of capital for capitalist society, since they put their small, carefully acquired savings into the bank or invested them in stocks and shares. This was another reason why they had no desire for revolutionary change which would put their savings at risk.

Hoarding characters also emerged at another social level in the late nineteenth century. Exploitative characters at home and abroad needed men with money to back them and to invest in their enterprises. Society produced hoarders of money and property who would fill this role, as merchant bankers.

The marketing character is the next of those proposed by Fromm in his early writings. A trendy through and through, the marketing character is neither this, that nor anything in particular, but only what is currently fashionable. The hoarder finds change difficult, but the marketing character lives by change, becoming what society and the times require.

Marketing characters resemble Freud's phallic personality, who is always something of a conformist. Like their clothes, cars, feelings, opinions and actions, their personality is just another commodity to be marketed and sold. If no one buys them they feel valueless, like a young person who is never invited to a party. On the positive side marketing characters are tolerant, sociable, open-minded, willing to try anything new. By remaining a product that others want, they avoid loneliness and insignificance. While they stay the brand that sells, they feel worth while, and loneliness and lack of meaning are kept at bay. If they fail to find the right image when society changes, they soon go out of fashion and, like Willy Loman in Arthur Miller's *Death of a Salesman*, no one attends their funeral.

The marketing character's strategy is to conform and be like everyone else – or, rather, everyone who counts. When it was fashionable to be radical and left wing, Dr Howard Kirk, Malcolm Bradbury's History Man, was radical and left wing. But times change; when reaction sets in, Dr Kirk becomes a Conservative. In conforming I am like everyone else, which solves the problem of being free, separate and lonely. Conformity wipes out any alarming difference between myself and others: 'See how nice I am – in fact, just like you.' What conformity makes me may be reasonable and decent if based on the right people and newspapers. But what I become is not me. What are supposedly *my* acts, thoughts and feelings are not mine at all, since I am only conforming . . . to public opinion, mother, convention, duty. Dr Kirk was never a true radical, only a mirror of the times. The marketing character is a false solution because conformity destroys identity. The real Dr Kirk does not exist. Even in the short term I am in a state of permanent anxiety, having to be alert to the shifting expectations of others.

The marketing character is thoroughly modern. Thanks to the advances of technology, in the West we now produce in excess of our needs, and companies no longer require hard-working hoarders or maverick exploiters, or only a few. Selling has come to replace production as the key to economic success. What companies need is organization men and women to market and sell the company, the products and themselves. The marketing character is a product of modern consumer society.

Fromm regards these four characters as false solutions to the problem of human loneliness and insignificance. They all reject human freedom. The only satisfactory solution is the productive character who embraces freedom. But it is difficult for Fromm to give a precise account of the productive being, since this remains an ideal – what humans ought to become – and only few achieve it.

The productivity of the productive character emerges above all in love and work. This love relates to others, respects others, wants what is best for others as well as for oneself. In work, what matters is not what is made but the attitude towards it; the productive character may create great art or build a wall or type invoices, but the product is not important. The most important product of human productivity is the human self. What shapes the self is not having composed *The Ring* or built a wall or typed invoices but one's attitude to what one has done. Reason, spontaneity, caring, concern are among the elements of a productive character. It is related to Freud's genital personality, but again Fromm reverses Freud. The individual's creativeness and productivity are not the result of sexual competence, but the other way around: sexual competence is just one expression of productivity.

Productive characters have found the true solution to loneliness and insignificance. The solution lies not in rejecting freedom but in becoming oneself. This is achieved by a love that eliminates loneliness by having relationships with others but which at the same time remains free. It is achieved in creative work that realizes human potential, replaces insignificance with genuine power, and relates one truly to nature. The productive character embraces what Fromm calls the creative solution. Freedom is to be welcomed and embraced, but the loneliness, insignificance and lack of meaning that freedom threatens us with are avoided by uniting with others in spontaneous love and by working creatively. Love and work are the answer.

Where are productive characters to be found? What sort of cultures are likely to shape them? Productive individuals may be found anywhere since human beings are able to transcend the most limiting environments. But we are also made by society, and the sick societies we inhabit make sick people. Only sane societies would shape productive people, and we have yet to build sane societies to do this. For the present, productive characters are few and far between.

Modern men and women need to find meaning in their lives in a world where God is dead, without resorting to repressive ideologies or organizations. They have to find meaning in what they do and are, because, says Fromm, 'the meaning of life is living' and 'there is no meaning to life except the meaning man gives his life by the unfolding of his powers'. Productive characters are preoccupied with personal fulfilment, relate meaningfully to others, attend group therapy and consciousness-raising sessions, and want to feel good. 'Feeling good' is important and, in the absence of external values, is the only value left. Fromm's productive character is an account of what human beings should be, a model from modern psychology to replace the old ideals of religion.

But the productive character is vague, and at times Fromm seems to be proposing nothing more than a better class of hedonist. The productive character goes in for much psychological navel-contemplation ... how do I feel? ... do I feel good? ... am I fulfilled? Fromm appears to be saying: since God is dead, and without religious faith we do not know where to turn, let us cling to one another in brotherly and sisterly love, and work creatively. But having become a free productive character, what exactly am I to do? Common-sense critics might find such advice empty, preferring to have specific objectives and goals in their lives.

Productive people like Gandhi, Martin Luther King or Mother Teresa do not live for the sake of living itself but for goals and objectives. All three would think it absurd that they should do what they do in order to fulfil themselves, to make themselves feel good. They have definite goals: equality, getting rid of oppression, eliminating racial discrimination, feeding the hungry, preaching God's word. It is unlikely that they or anyone else would become productive personalities without aims outside themselves. It is because Fromm can find no absolute values or external goals that he resorts to emphasizing the style, manner and spontaneity with which things are done. With the productive character it is rather like the song: 'It ain't what you do, it's the way that you do it'. But what is one to do? Smash windows? Beat up old ladies? Are there really no external criteria by which to judge the value of anything? Is how it is done all that matters? If this is the case, what is wrong with smashing windows or beating up grannies, so long as one does it with style and spontaneously, and it makes one feel good?

Fromm's answer is that smashing windows, assaulting grannies and sexual violence are unloving acts that would not satisfy and fulfil. When anyone finds and expresses their true personality, acts and desires that are uncreative and full of hate have no place. Freud would disagree. Violence and dangerous sexuality are exactly what Freud would expect if we came out with what we really feel. Marcuse, a Marxist and a Freudian, in a bitter attack accused Fromm of neo-Freudian revisionism. Fromm's account certainly emphasizes mind, choice, personal relations, and characterizes love, ethical values and meaning in life as being especially human. Fromm's emphasis is at the expense of the Freudian stress on body, instinct and passion. What Marcuse attacks Fromm for is his dismissal of the hard reality of biology and its substitution by what Marcuse regards as a false spiritual dimension. Fromm certainly writes as if God is about to be mentioned on the next page, but He never is – except as 'God is the image of what man might become'.

According to Fromm, concerns such as love, human relations, culture, meaning in life are what make humans human, and what might make them happy. This contrasts with Freud who regards these higher activities as the very cause of human suffering: 'Neurosis is the price we pay for civilization.' For Fromm, these higher concerns are as important as bodily ones, particularly in modern industrial society where it is possible to satisfy everyone's material needs without difficulty. According to Fromm, human unhappiness arises because the individual's needs for love, personal relations, meaning in life, fulfilment, come into conflict with society. All that is necessary for human happiness is to change society slightly (get rid of exploitation, injustice, inequality, competition, repression) and let people be themselves, without pressure to conform and with opportunities for self-expression. Marxists like Marcuse dismiss Fromm contemptuously as a liberal. Freudians, believing that human beings have insatiable appetites, an unconscious, a death instinct and are capable of unimaginable violence, also regard Fromm's account as liberal nonsense.

Fromm's knowledge is extensive – history, religion, philosophy, sociology, psychology and, in particular, psycho-analysis. He regards his character types as based on the scientific analysis of psycho-analysis. But with the productive character that human beings *ought* to be, Fromm stops being the scientific psychologist to become the moralist. He claims that his productive character is based on the insights and understanding that scientific psycho-analysis provides; but it seems to be just a point of view, with no particular data as evidence.

Fromm gets away with it because there is nothing he says that any decent individual would object to. We should love one another, work, be rational, care, use our abilities to the full – and who would disagree? There is nothing new in this; common sense, informed by most religious traditions, has been suggesting it for centuries. Where are the insights and revelations on the human condition Fromm promised psycho-analysis would provide? And though Fromm's exhortations are acceptable, their preoccupation with abstractions even threatens to make them meaningless. Loving an abstraction – humanity, the oppressed, women (if one is male), the under-privileged – may be important, but it is not difficult. Equally important, and more difficult, is loving a flawed embodiment of such an abstraction, like Peter, Jane, Winston. Fromm believes that love, concern, compassion should be all-embracing, but they are in danger of becoming empty if they are not also particularized in specific human beings.

Fromm regards work as important. But his suggestion that people should work because they enjoy it would have been thought ludicrous at most times and in most places. Work has been unpleasant for the greater part of history, and human beings have worked simply in order to survive. Any dignity or meaning in work has come from surrounding beliefs – 'Though your labour is painful, yet it means you do penance for your sins ... you are doing the work of God's redemption ... you are blessed in God's eyes ... to work is to pray'.

It would be nice if we all had interesting and fulfilling jobs, and some people have; but many find their job boring and work only out of necessity. Some who find value in their work still do so because of beliefs, though these beliefs may have changed: work is the service of others, or is building the new capitalist or socialist Jerusalem. But for Fromm such justifications are irrelevant; the only value work would have in the sane society would be its intrinsic satisfaction. What should be marvellous about your job and mine is the work itself! Fromm takes this one step further. It is only your work – together with your love – that can give your life meaning. But work cannot carry such a burden of justifying and giving value to our lives.

And Fromm does not explain *how* we are to work creatively, love, embrace freedom, care, fulfil ourselves, be responsible and rational. We are simply to do so. How this is to be done in our daily lives or what it means for bringing up our children, Fromm does not say. Carl Rogers' account is equally humanistic but at least he does suggest techniques to help in therapy; Fromm says little about therapy.

Fromm's view, that human beings are free but that freedom depends on the conflicting forces being balanced, was outlined earlier. Neither the aged Faust nor an elderly St Francis are likely to be free. What freedom exists for the rest of us is limited to the alternatives available. But the freedom which interests Fromm is not the trivial choice between tieing up the left or the right shoe-lace first. He is concerned with moral decisions, with choosing good over evil, love before hate, and independence rather than subservience. Unlike atheistic existentialists, he does not hold that suicide, loving our neighbour, stealing from the blind, giving to the poor, assaulting granny, are all valid expressions of freedom, provided they are unforced. Fromm resembles Rogers in believing that the individual is really free only when choosing what is right and good. Freedom is about following reason, acting in the interests of ourself and other people, doing what is for the well-being of ourself and others. His view is like the medieval notion of an all-loving God who is utterly free but who has no choice to do other than what He does, which is right and good.

As a liberal, Fromm believes that education will help us achieve the true freedom of choosing what is good. He seems to hold 'there is no sin but ignorance'. As a therapist he believes that with awareness and insight we are more likely to do what is good. Knowing what good and right and wrong actually are, which forces – particularly which unconscious forces – affect us, which options are open to us and what their likely consequences are, will help us to be free.

But if we are able to choose only from existing alternatives, how can anything new originate, like an original scientific theory or a new dance step? Fromm describes the productive character as possible only through a 'free decision of the heart'. But his account emphasizes that human beings are shaped by economic forces and are a product of society's values and beliefs, all operating through class and family relationships. He does not explain how, in this welter of influences, free choice remains possible, nor what it is.

It looks as if we are heading once more for what in *The Heart of Man* Fromm 'called "soft determinism" and according to which it is consistent to believe in determinism and human freedom. While my position is more akin to "soft" than "hard" determinism it is not that of the former either.' But despite his denial, a form of soft determinism is what Fromm, like Rogers, leaves us with. Fromm seems to be saying, for example, that in choosing to be dependent on others, the receptive personality is acting in character: 'That was just like him.' In manipulating other people for her own ends, an exploitative personality is merely acting in the way her character is shaped: 'It was typical of her.' This is the soft determinism that Fromm adopts to qualify the idea that human beings are free. But soft determinism is no solution, since it is clear to common sense that in a given situation, a particular person is ultimately free or not free, one or the other, not both. With many qualifications, Fromm opts for free choice without explaining where the capacity for choice originates in the individual or how it operates. And if, as his historical approach appears to suggest, the capacity for free choice emerged during human evolution, he does not demonstrate how it did.

Fromm has to come down on the side of free choice because, if humans are moral beings, we must be free – to choose good or bad, right or wrong. And Fromm continually stresses our moral nature. There is a voice in us, he says, 'the voice of our true selves which summons us back to ourselves, to live productively, to develop fully and harmoniously – that is, *to become what we potentially are*.' The voice distinguishes between good and bad, right and wrong.

For Fromm, behaving morally means being true to our human potential: '"good" is what is good for man and "evil" what is detrimental to man.' I try to do right because right is good for me, and I try not to do wrong because wrong is bad for me. Acting in my own best interest, I act also in the best interest of others. When I do what is right by loving and acting in the interest of others, I am doing what fulfils my true potential and is right for me. This is the supposed revelation of psycho-analysis – or rather, Fromm's version, since he contends that Freud got it wrong about conflict.

Human conflict arises, Fromm believes, only because society is badly organized, and with the insights of psycho-analysis we can reorganize society on the right moral lines. In this new ethic, man and woman become the measure of all things ...

'good in humanistic ethics is the affirmation of life, the unfolding of man's powers ... Evil constitutes the crippling of man's powers.' And what we ought to be and do Fromm has expressed in the productive character. But its 'oughts' of love, care, concern, responsibility and the rest are nothing new; they are to be found in the Christian New Testament and in the liberal tradition of all great religions. Again, where are the insights Fromm promised from psycho-analysis?

If we interpret Fromm's '"good" is what is good for man' broadly, it is empty, but if we take it narrowly, it seems nonsense. When Oates walked out into the snow so that Scott and the others might survive, in what sense was Oates's act good for himself? His death was inevitable, so in the narrow sense nothing good could come of it for himself. In the broader interpretation, his act may have meant that he was a better man in those few moments between leaving the tent and dying. This may have made him healthier psychologically as he declined physically in the intense cold. But it is absurd to suggest that this was Oates's reason for leaving the tent – he did it to save the others, not for his own good. If what Oates did has any meaning, it does so because of moral standards that our common sense grasps but cannot explain or justify: 'Greater love than this no man has, that he lay down his life for a friend'. Sacrificing your life for others is a good act – it just is.

Most of Fromm's values add nothing to a common sense that has been informed by liberal religious traditions. At the same time, his values lack the power that the idea of God or of moral law as part of human nature gives to a value. When he attempts to justify moral acts, which for common sense need no justification, he resorts to verbal juggling. 'God is the image of what man might become', and 'there is no meaning to life except the meaning man gives his life by the unfolding of his powers'.

To suggest that Oates walked out into the snow because the act was good for him and made a productive man of him turns him into a sort of hedonist. Ironically – since Fromm is trying to raise human dignity – such a view diminishes what Oates did. It is as if knowing the significance of his act gave him a moral glow that compensated for the cold, the fear, the lonely death, the awareness of the pain it would cause loved-ones in England! Oates walked out into the snow against his inclinations because he believed it was the right thing to do. Sacrificing one's life for others is a good act; it just is – there is nothing more one can add. The suggestion that scientific psycho-analysis provides a basis for human values is nonsense, and Fromm certainly provides no evidence in support of the idea.

Fromm sees human beings as naturally moral and innately inclined to good, as Carl Rogers does. But he does confront human destructiveness in a way that Rogers fails to do. Fromm's view is that hatred and destructiveness result when the human struggle to live and to act creatively is frustrated. Hamlet is thwarted by oppressive patriarchal life at the castle and the sick feudal society he lives in. It is not in Hamlet but in the state of Denmark that something is rotten. When his struggle to become what he truly is – free, productive, good – gets frustrated, it can end only in tragedy.

But hatred and destructiveness come second, only after the original impulse to love and to create is blocked. It happens not just to Hamlet but to everyone, and it happens because all societies are unfit for human habitation. All societies prevent people from achieving their potential; they twist love into hate; and they make our inclination to live morally turn into violence and destructiveness, like a prince changing into a frog. This is the Fall of Man the Bible describes; and it happens repeatedly, as every generation is damaged and distorted by the sick, insane society it is born in. Some societies are less damaging than others, but all frustrate human potential and make people flawed, mean, evil. 'If life's tendency to grow, to be lived, is thwarted, the energy thus blocked undergoes a process of change and is transformed into life-destructive energy. *Destructiveness is the outcome of unlived life*.' What has blocked the human potential of twentieth-century man and woman, and made them the way they are, is patriarchal competitive capitalism.

When Freud introduced the death instinct in his later writings to explain human violence, he placed it on an equal footing with the life instinct. When Fromm in his later writings introduced necrophilia, the 'love of the dead', and biophilia, 'the love of life', he did not regard them as equals. For Fromm 'the love of life' comes first, and life is what human beings are equipped for. The 'love of the dead' is merely a sick distortion which emerges when the impulse to life is blocked. The great refusal in the Garden of Eden meant the species separated from nature – it was cast out of paradise – and became human; but the rebellion has to be repeated in every lifetime. Each of us has to break free – from God in the Garden, from the Grand Inquisitor of culture, from the collective ant-hill of society, from incestuously inclined mothers – to become truly human. Whichever womb it is, we have to escape from it if it is not to become our tomb. Mother, family, society, mother-country, blood, race are our genesis, the source of life, but any of them can turn into an octopus that smothers and stifles us.

It is the failure to break incestuous bonds and become individual that is the root cause of Fromm's 'love of the dead', that 'passion to transform that which is alive into something unalive; to destroy for the sake of destruction ... to tear apart living structure'. This is the late anal character in pathological form. In its full malignant destructiveness it is Hitler's enjoyment of torture, wanting the bomb to drop, or George Orwell's future in *1984* of 'a boot stamping on a human face – for ever'.

Free choice has its place in such destructiveness, though Fromm remains vague about this. However, Fromm is clear about what causes destructiveness, whether it be Hitler's or the modest disruptiveness of the late anal character or even that of Shakespeare's Hamlet. The play ends with bodies all over the stage, not primarily because of Hamlet's anger with the uncle who had murdered his father; it ends in violence because Hamlet cannot separate himself from his father and mother, even though one of them is dead. Hamlet has not grown up and become free, fully human and alive by standing up to his parents, and the result is destructiveness.

Human destructiveness manifests itself also as sadism. Sadism appears in many forms: bullying in the playground, sarcasm in the classroom, wife-beating, torture, Stalin's delight in ordering the execution of the friend or the wife of a subordinate. There may be innate factors in sadism, and personal experience of terrifying and arbitrary punishment may play its part. School bullies are often on the receiving end of bullying at home, and wife-beaters usually have fathers who beat their mothers. But Fromm regards the influence of the wider society as important, and a society where one class or group dominates and exploits another is a breeding-ground for sadists. Like 'the love of the dead', sadism is secondary because humans are innately equipped with the potential for care, creativity and love. Sadism is adopted only as a last resort, a particularly unpleasant solution to loneliness and insignificance which emerges when societies make truly human solutions impossible.

Fromm is clear: the purpose of existence is love, doing good, genuine relationships and productive work. This is our nature. When men and women are evil and destructive, it is only because their potential to mature into free creative beings is frustrated by sick societies. Human evil and destructiveness are only 'the outcome of unlived life'; when we have built sane societies, our full potential will begin to be realized. Within the limits of the human condition imposed by unchanging constraints like death, all problems are solvable – by technology and now more importantly by social and psychological science. Fromm affirms: 'I believe in the perfectibility of man.'

Though a neo-Freudian, Fromm – in contrast to Freud himself – provides us with an optimistic view of human beings. At the same time he has made us aware that we are not as fond of freedom as we would like to believe. He has enabled us to see that authoritarian ideologies, repressive regimes, totalitarian political movements, uncaring commercial companies are not unfortunate accidents of our times, but in part are the result of our reluctance to be free and responsible. Fromm has shown how the free choice that we have, even when embraced, is not total. Class, society, economic structure, and ideas, usually working through the family, shape us and limit our freedom. And Fromm has not ignored human violence and destructiveness but has suggested how they occur when human growth is frustrated, often by external circumstances.

Out of this awareness of how family, relationships, the economic structure, society, and the current coinage of ideas and values shape human beings, Fromm has created a useful classification of personality. In this system, human freedom and choice are not ignored. And Fromm suggests that it is because such fluid factors shape personality that personality develops differently in different social classes and different historical situations. This leads us to ask: what is our situation? Human beings have never been at home in the world, and with the death of God and the decline of religion we seem now totally without any roof over our heads. Fromm has seen that 'Man does not live by bread alone' and needs meaning in life. Fromm's solution, that society should be so structured as to enable people to find love, creative work and meaning in their lives, is useful – if inadequate and rather obvious. More original is his realization that, besides love and relationships, people need to be separate and independent and free if they are to become truly human.

In his approach to the problem of mind Fromm begins from an evolutionary standpoint. Human beings are strange in many ways, but particularly odd is their ambivalent relationship with the natural world from which they emerged. In the course of evolution the power of animal instinct has declined, while the higher processes of reason, memory and imagination have increased. Freud knew this but stressed that animal instinct remains a powerful force in human beings. But for Fromm this evolutionary development of higher processes has transformed everything; and crucial for the human being has been the development of an awareness of one's self as something separate. The awareness of a self meant that mind and consciousness had arrived, and human beings had become separate from nature. Though separate, they remained subject to its laws, apart from nature while still part of nature. There was now a new species on Earth, an animal that not only knows but knows it knows. With human consciousness a quite different type of animal had arrived, part of nature but transcending nature. Evolution had produced a freak because life had become aware of itself – but Fromm does not explain how this happened.

It is our freak condition – part of but apart from nature – which is the origin of so much human anguish. 'It is wonderful to look upon the things of the world,' said the Buddha, 'and terrible to be them.' It is also the cause of our strange experience of seeming to live in two worlds, material and spirit, body and mind. In Fromm's account, we have consciousness and mind which are partly responsible for making us do what we do. There is nothing startling in this and it would be part of any common-sense view of human beings. But though Fromm puts mind and consciousness firmly in an evolutionary context, nowhere does he account for their emergence.

For Freud we begin only as instinct and body and, from this, mind emerges. But Fromm does not see mind, consciousness, creativity, our need and capacity for love and human relationships as coming second. With Fromm mind is not determined by biology, but what we do with our body is partly decided by our mind. Mind comes first. Fromm, we have suggested, writes as if God is about to be appealed to on the next page; and his emphasis on the higher human processes recalls Genesis and God breathing spirit into matter. But Fromm is no dualist and does not believe that besides body there is soul or spirit. Like Freud he holds we are nothing but bodies . . . and minds!

Fromm does not adopt Freud's account of mind and consciousness emerging from bodies in the course of each individual development. In Fromm's account our minds may not precede our bodies into our mothers' wombs, but they seem to emerge with them. So what is mind, if spirit does not exist? How do mind and consciousness relate to the body which they affect so powerfully? Where does our need and capacity to relate to other people come from? Who or what does the relating?

Mind, conscious I, and the person that thinks, remembers, imagines, that needs to relate to others, to be free and to work productively, that is moral in nature . . . are real enough in Fromm's account. But he does not explain how they originate, nor even what they are.

Chapter Six

MERELY PLAYERS:

The social behaviourism of role theory and G. H. Mead

All the world's a stage,
And all the men and women merely players.
                    Shakespeare: *As You Like It*, Act II, sc. vii

If you want to go to university, make sure you are not born the daughter of a labourer, a window-cleaner or a kitchen-hand. There are almost no women with fathers in social class five among graduates from British universities. If your father is an unskilled worker and you are male, your chances of getting to university improve only slightly. Even when IQs at the age of eleven are the same, the children of unskilled and semi-skilled workers are less likely to end up with 'O'- and 'A'-level passes and degrees than those from a higher social class. Your best bet is to be born the son of a father in a profession.

People's lives are decided by their social position – this is the view of role theory. There is no need to resort to Freudian super-egos, Skinner's rewards and punishments, the Rogerian self or Fromm's problems of relationships in order to account for the behaviour of human beings. All we need do is look at their sex, social class, family, religion, age. We are born male or female . . . black, white, yellow . . . in a certain family in a particular class . . . Protestant, Hindu or whatever . . . and we are a certain age. We have no choice about any of this – but, as role theory demonstrates, it decides our lives.

Even the jobs we seem to deserve credit for are not ours because of application and talent. I am now qualified as a doctor; but being male with a doctor for a father (and one who could afford the right school) helped me to get to medical college. Having become a doctor (or docker) decides the rest:

how I dress, talk, think, vote, my interests, my health, the sort of person I marry, how well my children will do at school, what I will die of. In the account that role theory provides, human beings exist in societies and behave the way they do because of society. We are actors in roles not of our choosing and with no alternative but to play them. Even if we quit normal society, there are ready-made roles for us to drop into, such as tramp, hippie, dissident. We are born into societies that are organized into roles, and these immediately make clear what is expected of us. What is expected depends on whether I am male or female, white or black, the son of a doctor or a docker, a Smith or a Smythe, the daughter of agnostics or of devout Catholics.

But social behaviourism goes further and states that the influence of human society is even more fundamental – it makes us human. The Indian Wolf Children, reared by wolves, howled but did not talk, moved awkwardly on all fours, could mix with wolves but not with people.

Role theory makes us realize that the network we are enmeshed in is vast. Son, brother, friend, nephew, schoolboy, adolescent, doctor, husband, son-in-law, father, householder, neighbour, member of the local rotary club, parishioner, Conservative Party member . . . not only do I play many parts but each involves other people, who expect something of me, whether as son, brother, doctor, husband, neighbour or whatever. As a doctor, there are patients, medical colleagues, non-medical colleagues, professional organizations, the local authority, pharmaceutical firms . . . The knowledge required for the many roles I play is so extensive and complex that I could not possibly have worked it out for myself. I ought to be grateful to society for doing it for me. On the other hand, society begins to look less like a theatre, with me and others on stage, and more like an enormous prison.

The prison is not obvious, but it exists and there is no escape. There is no 'outside' I can climb over the wall and escape to; there is only the prison. Once you are born and inside, others will make sure you behave as you are supposed to, and eventually you in your turn will do the same to others. There are ways

. . . ridicule, contempt, ostracism and, in the last resort, force – but force rarely has to be used. In spite of complaints about crime waves, what is surprising about society is how safe it is and the fact that most of us can walk home at night without being mugged, raped or assaulted. Force rarely has to be used to make society safe, because we conform without fuss. In the role theory view, there is no violent conflict between society and our bodily needs, as Freud believed, because the pressure on us to play our parts is considerable and we learn them quickly.

Children learn particularly quickly. Gentle pressure is applied, and little Jane understands that girls are gentle and young John discovers that boys do not cry. Beginning with parents, then with brothers and sisters, later with teachers and other adults, children learn the roles appropriate to their sex, colour, age, family, class, religion. This continues into adult life, when any squeamish nurse or medical student is 'socialized' into not fainting at the sight of blood or while witnessing what goes on in the operating theatre. The toolmaker who is promoted to foreman and to the staff lunch-room changes his daily paper and his attitudes to those more favourable to management. Role theory explains why we live normal lives. From womb to tomb we are influenced by our fellow actors and we act the way they expect us to.

Yet some crime, conflict and non-conformity exist – how is this possible if we are all such conformists? Society dictates what goals we should strive for; in our society, they are success, money and material possessions. If we are born into a situation and class society approves of, society provides socially approved means for achieving these goals. If this is not enough for some, there is always white-collar crime such as tax evasion and fraud to turn to. If we are born in circumstances society approves of less, society does not make available legitimate means to success, money and possessions, while still confirming that they are what matter; one option is to turn to crime or alternative life-styles or some form of rebellion. According to social behaviourism, society creates conflict, non-conformity and crime by telling us what goals to strive for, but not making it possible for everyone to achieve them.

In sport, supporters, managers and financial rewards tell players that what counts is winning. With such an emphasis on ends and (with footballers) goals, quite reasonably players bother less about whether the means are within the rules; they question referees' decisions on line balls, they make unfair tackles and resort to professional fouls. Role theory can explain conflict in society without resorting to Freud's savage instincts inside us.

When there is conflict within people, it is also because of our roles. Sometimes what is expected of us is not clear; these days, Mr Jones does not know if as a father he should be letting his son go his own way or insist that he be in by midnight. There may be competing demands in a role and it may be unclear which should be given priority. As a lecturer, Mrs Smith is supposed to teach, do administrative work, carry out research, and these all compete for her time. But she has not been told which has priority and, as there are only so many hours in the day, this puts her under strain. Worse than unclear and competing expectations are conflicting ones. Mr Jones's son says: 'Get off my back, Dad, I'm sixteen now!' The boy's grandfather says: 'You need to be firmer with that boy!' The mother says: 'You should take more interest in him but not boss him around so much.' There is another kind of strain when the roles we occupy do not mesh: a working mother may have a demanding family as well as a demanding job, and a Roman Catholic nurse may work in a hospital where abortions are performed.

Most of us are under the illusion that societies are composed of individuals joined together. Role theory sees that this is like believing that when a woman called Ophelia and a man called Hamlet, together with his mother, Gertrude, and some others, come together, we have a play called *Hamlet*. But the play exists first and it existed long before the present cast arrived and will be there long after they are dead and gone. Hamlets and Ophelias come and go, but the play survives. In real life, society and culture come first and exist before the human actors. There is already a script and, though little has been written down, there are always the words and gestures of the other actors, usually the older and more experienced ones, to tell us what to say and do. Heaven help us if we fail to act on cue and so spoil their performances! Theatrical props of factory and workbench, of office and office furniture, of classroom, of bed and bedroom, pub and bus-stop, cue us in to the appropriate performance. According to whichever play we are in, we find ourselves on stage with different actors – wife or colleague or neighbour – with whom to interact appropriately.

Society's roles and expectations may be outside us to begin with, but eventually they end up inside. We stop acting and become the parts we are playing. An intelligent secretary, more capable than the manager she is secretary to, dutifully performs her subordinate role. But society decrees that men should be managers and women should be secretaries, so eventually we take society inside us. Our typecasting (or imprisonment in our roles) goes further and the secretary *enjoys* the subordinate role she *has* to fill. A few years ago, English schoolgirls did not perform as well at school as their brothers. However, they did not fret and fume since 'Be good, sweet maid, and let who will be clever' were the stage directions. The strength of their performance lay in feelings and personal relations and these would emerge in a different, domestic play. They knew they would end up as society said they should, in parts they were best fitted for, as good wives and mothers.

In the end, we *want* to act in the way we have to, which is why so little force is necessary in society. We may begin by playing our roles but, like any competent actor, we end up living, breathing and being them. In saying this, social behaviourism is moving from the role theory account of the effect on people of being in society, and is emphasizing rather the effect of society being in people. Society becomes internalized in human beings; people end up with society inside them.

This view, that human beings become the parts they are playing, is developed in George Herbert Mead's symbolic interactionism. The game of life described by Mead is played, like the role theory one, with rules that already exist. In any culture there is agreement about rules and a world-taken-for-granted, which other cultures may not share. When Captain Cook arrived in the South Seas, the islanders took what they fancied from his ship and he concluded that they did not think stealing was wrong. The difference went deeper because, in a society where everything is owned by the whole community, there *can be* no idea of what 'stealing' is.

In our culture it seems obvious that every event has a material cause, that work is a good thing and everyone wants a job, that all men are equal. But such views are merely part of our culture and are 'obvious' because society shapes what we believe. Opposite views have been held in the past and still are today. In less scientific cultures no one believes that every event has a material cause, since it is obvious that God and spirits intervene in human affairs. Many societies look on work as a burden, to be avoided if possible. At other times the idea that all men are equal was regarded as nonsense. The extremes of inequality, of oppression by colonialization and slavery, have been practised by apparently reasonable men. But within a particular culture we share with others this world-taken-for-granted.

Two old-age pensioners are talking in a pub and one asks: 'Would you like to hear the story of my life?' 'No,' says the other, 'it's probably the same as mine.' The second pensioner has got the point of social behaviourism. Living in the same society and class, their lives are likely to be very similar.

As children and adults, we learn the views of those around us and accept the same world-taken-for-granted. When we are children, the view others have of us personally is particularly important because it becomes the basis for our own view of our self. The views other people have of us we accept and adopt as our own identity and our very self. In Mead's account, society and other people exist first, and then the human self develops out of society and other people's views.

The human self emerges in three stages. First, there is a preparatory stage, in which the infant meaninglessly imitates others. Baby waves arms to copy Daddy's wave of good-bye or looks at the paper because this is what Mummy does. There is no understanding, and the infant is only mimicking externals. Next comes the play stage, where the infant goes on doing what others do, but now with glimmerings of understanding. At this stage, children play the parts of others who are important to them such as mother, father, milkman, brother, sister. By acting the roles of these *significant others*, the child develops an awareness of what they expect of him or her. There is a set of expectations from each of them: Mummy–Jane, Daddy–Jane, brother–Jane, milkman–Jane. Jane puts together an appropriate self for each set of expectations, one for what Mummy expects, another for what Daddy expects, and so on. At this stage a child has many 'selfs', each with its own behaviour, one for each of these significant others he or she knows. At this time a child refers to itself using the third person – Jane loves Mummy, Jane is angry with teddy – as if its own identity had not been grasped. Some people think, among them many Buddhists, that the adult is like this, many self-ed, with selfs layered like the skins of an onion.

But Mead believed that the development of the self continues to a third, and final, game stage. As the child finds itself more and more often in situations in which a number of people are present, it forms a common self to cope with what they all expect. This is possible because what different people expect of a particular child has many features in common. These common features may exist because the child is male or female, black or white, or because in that particular culture toddlers are expected to be quiet, passive and obedient. Perhaps for some reason everyone expects this particular infant to be amusing. So the child moves from many selfs, each appropriate for one particular *significant other*, to a single core self which meets the expectations of a composite *generalized other*.

In Virginia Woolf's novel, the eponymous Mrs Dalloway sits before a mirror putting on her make-up for her party that evening. But the reader realizes she is not just putting on a face but pulling her 'self' together. At this game stage, each of us develop a Jane or John for all seasons and situations. What began out in society is now in me ... is Me. Unlike Mrs Dalloway in front of the mirror, I no longer need to make an effort. I am naturally myself now, experiencing this self of mine as unique and inevitable. But this self of mine was originally put together by society.

With this self I take on board society's values and views

about the way the world is, its world-taken-for-granted. I know that my daughter's illness was caused by an evil spirit, or by a virus, or by the malice of an enemy – whatever my culture says. I know now that all men are equal or unequal, that God does or does not exist, that work is good or is something to be avoided. I know what a fork is for, how one should react to a policeman or to the death of a relative. In some cultures it seems natural and inevitable that people want to improve themselves and earn more and more. In other societies all that people want is enough to go round. Culture decides what is true and right for us, and it becomes almost impossible to question its world-taken-for-granted unless one is aware of alternative world-views. It is for this reason that totalitarian regimes attempt to restrict communication with other societies.

It does not end there; having been made by society, the self needs society for it to go on existing. Mrs Dalloway's personality at the party depends as much on the other party-goers as on herself. Being a mother has been important to Mrs Smith, but her children have grown up and left home, making her role of mother obsolete; now her very self and identity are at risk. As a lecturer, my self depends as much on my students as on any effort of mine. If they talked through my lectures, got up and walked out, stopped attending, my lecturer self would be at risk.

It might be objected that this lecturer self, and other selfs such as those of brother and husband, are only on the surface. My real self lies beneath. But to Mead's social behaviourism an unobservable 'real self beneath' would not be scientific, and sounds a shade mystical. The only selfs that exist are those we know about at first hand, Mrs Dalloway's at the party or mine in the lecture hall; and these are made and sustained by others. We are social through and through, and whether my self continues to exist depends on recognition and acknowledgement by other people. The power of solitary confinement to strip away beliefs, values and identity itself is evidence of this. A political prisoner in solitary confinement will eventually talk with anyone, even the prison guards and representatives of the regime he hates, to keep himself sane and human.

Even a sick self, say a schizophrenic one, is created by society – by parents, work, marriage. Subsequently the routines of mental hospital confirm the 'fact' of our being mentally ill. If I was not mentally ill when I entered hospital, everything there would quickly make me so. Criminals are made and kept criminal by those round them, in the same way that others are shaped into law-abiding citizens. What is the point of trying to get someone to change his criminal ways if he goes on mixing with other criminals who daily confirm his old-lag identity? People change only when the situation they are in becomes different; and schizophrenics and criminals change, for better or worse, only when their circumstances change. Every year thousands of alert and interested young children enter primary school. Eleven or so years later, they leave school with 'slow' ... 'dull, not interested' ... 'tries, but of limited ability' on their reports, and by now these comments are true. Some obscure social process in the classroom has turned keen, bright infants into unresponsive, dull teenagers. I am and become what others expect of me ... mentally ill, criminal, stupid. We are back to society as a prison, but the prison is now inside me. In the symbolic interactionist view, the prison is my self.

If society first builds the prison, we end up being our own jailers and we throw away the key. Eventually we are not only what society wants us to be but are happy to be that way. A mother enjoys caring for her baby not because of some fictitious maternal instinct but because this is expected of her, and what is expected of her becomes her self. 'Our nature is such,' said Pascal, 'that if you sufficiently impress upon someone that he is a fool he will believe you.' A young male, fiercely combative at work and on the squash court – such is his macho self – revels in his competitiveness. Our performance has become the real thing and, like Hamlet, we resent any suggestion that we are pretending: 'Seems, madam! Nay, it is; I know not "seems".' And there is much to be said for prison, since it provides us with a self, an identity, and it makes us human. Look how the Indian Wolf Children turned out! Consider how people disintegrate in solitary confinement!

But according to symbolic interactionism, the pensioner we

overheard earlier was not entirely correct: the lives of the two pensioners would be similar but not identical, because there are chinks in the prison wall. Though we live in societies with a consensus about the world and ourselves, in the end we make our own interpretation. Things about us do not exist with labels attached to them to tell us what they are. No God has gone around naming every object and saying what it is for. A flower in his vegetable patch is a weed to a vegetable-grower; for a botanist, it may be a rare species of flora; for the poet, a symbol of beauty and transience. One person looks at the National Front and sees a bunch of toughs, another sees true patriots, another alienated youth. It is human beings who name everything and give an account of what each is for. The names and accounts people give vary from culture to culture and from individual to individual.

Society comes first, then comes the self made out of the roles we play. But there are different ways of playing our parts; even if the events of the pensioners' lives were identical, how they interpret and play them could be different. Mind makes this possible. According to Mead, first there is society, then there is self, then comes mind.

For radical behaviourists like Skinner, what causes human behaviour is outside: the carrot, the stick and the electric prod of reinforcement. But according to Mead's social behaviourism (and common sense), something important happens inside. When I take down the lead to take the dog out, and the dog barks, Skinner's account might do for the dog, but it won't for me. Skinner's account is inadequate to account for me because human beings have minds. The pigeon does not peck the disc with the intention of getting food, but I took down the lead because I intend to take the dog for a walk. The rat does not come to a halt in a maze and try to work out how the left turn ahead relates to what it is looking for – but this is what a human being would do, and car-drivers do it all the time. According to Mead (and common sense), there is meaning in what humans do, and they do things for a purpose in a way that dogs, pigeons, rats and even Skinner's human beings do not. According to symbolic interactionism, each of us is able to interpret our part differently, while remaining faithful to the script. One portrayal of Hamlet brings out his sadness, another his anger, another his loneliness. Even if society did cast the pensioners in identical roles, they can play them differently because human beings have minds.

An angry dog bares its teeth, and some other animal knows it will get bitten if it does not back off or submit. The other animal knows this because baring the teeth is the beginning of a bite. Human beings sometimes bare their teeth to show they are angry, but language does it better. Cutting words or a biting remark communicate our hostility with more accuracy and detail. The novelist Henry James speaks of '. . . the substitute of the few placed articulate words for the cry or the thump or the hug'. Mead believes that language developed through the long period of our evolution because it is more useful. Language works better than a gesture like baring one's teeth.

It needs to be said immediately that this is no explanation. To explain the evolutionary emergence of language, an account would need to spell out in detail the stages of development, their nature, how they occurred, what caused them, and even provide supporting evidence. To say that we became capable of biting words and cutting remarks because they are more useful than baring our teeth may be sound evolutionary theory, and may even be true, but is inadequate as scientific explanation.

However language did come about, Mead sees it as an important difference between the animal and the human. The dog's baring of its teeth requires no interpretation on the part of others, but language does. There is nothing about the letters 'r' and 'e' and 'd' that makes them, when put together, inevitably mean a certain colour. Symbolic interactionism stresses that human communication is largely symbolic, and that symbols such as letters of the alphabet have to be learnt and interpreted. There is nothing about the colour 'red' that makes it mean 'Stop', and yellow or green would have done just as well. But just as the colour red needs to be interpreted at the traffic-lights, so even other people's physical gestures have to be interpreted. Flicking the chin, clenching the fist, crossing one's fingers, thumbs up, may mean good luck, everything's fine, or they may be a slur, a sexual invitation or even a sexual insult; it depends on the culture. Unlike the dog's bared teeth, you will not know what certain combinations of letters, a gesture or a red light at the traffic signals mean, unless you have first learnt or been told.

Mead points out that the symbols human beings use most are words; and words mean something only if humans have first agreed what they mean. *Knabe, garçon, boy*, mean what they do because human beings have agreed about these sounds and squiggles, and so can interpret them. But interpretations can vary and be slightly different. Actors interpret Hamlet's words and gestures differently. Actors, whether on stage or in real life, are not passive with their scripts; they can and do give a personal touch to words, gestures and stage directions, particularly those relating to their own roles. Mind makes this possible.

Put a rat at the start of a maze and it immediately bolts off down an alley. Researchers are tempted to grab the rat and say, 'Hey, have a look first,' because this is what a human would do. A human would 'have a look first' because humans have minds. A radical behaviourist like Skinner denies mind; but for a social behaviourist like Mead, mind is real. The same tune on an electric guitar is music to the young guitarist, a racket to his middle-aged father, and interesting discords to a trained musician. What Mead sees as coming between the same notes and the different reactions of pleasure, irritation and interest is mind. In Mead's account, there is only one independent existing reality and that is body but mind is real too.

Mead addresses himself to the question of how mind originated and, as with language, he points out that mind is useful. Humans, on the lookout for a particular place, do not streak off like the rat at the start of the maze but stop, note the names of roads, think, reflect, consult a map. Only humans have brains large enough for this level of mental activity. Given the existence of this big brain, mind will develop for the good evolutionary reason that it is useful. Mind increases our chances of survival. Unlike the rat in the maze, men and women hesitate and reflect before they act because this means they are more likely to find what they are looking for. Mind has developed because with mind humans are more likely to survive.

Pigeons, cats, rats and humans drink water rather than oil, they all avoid enemies and fire, and they do not eat anything poisonous. With rats, cats and pigeons, there is little choice because what they do is the result of programming by evolution or conditioning by the environment's reward and punishment. But the adjustment of human beings to the external world is more free and deliberate; they find their way to their destination by looking first, consulting street-maps and names, and thinking for a while before hurrying on. People work out in advance what might happen by trying it out in their minds.

How did mind come about? Like the rat, cat and pigeon, our animal ancestors were programmed by evolution to communicate by grunt, gesture, squeak or whatever. They got across to others Help me . . . Follow me . . . Keep your distance . . . I am about to attack . . . using noise and gesture. When pre-human animals grunted or gesticulated to communicate with others, eventually they grasped what it was they *themselves* were saying. When an animal ancestor caressed his mate, he eventually got to know as well as she did what he was after. When some pre-human mother bared her teeth at a predator who came too close, she eventually knew as well as the predator what she intended to do if it came closer. Pre-human animals knowing what they themselves meant signalled the beginnings of mind. When the brain was big enough, grunt and gesture and eventually words communicated to grunter, gesticulator, speaker what it was that they *themselves* were saying. Mind began when in addressing another I was also addressing myself. When we arrive at a situation in which my external conversation with another (by gesture, grunt, words or whatever) is also an internal conversation with myself, we have mind.

What particularly helped was the arrival of language, which evolved, as we said, because words are more useful than cry, thump or hug. Language was particularly significant in the evolution of mind because with words we hear ourselves communicate. Humans have not developed the ability to talk because they can think, but the other way around: they have developed the ability to think because they can talk. First, there is society; then selfs emerge in society; when selfs in society communicate with each other and eventually with themselves, we have mind.

Mead's account of the origin of mind is ingenious and may be correct but, like his account of the origin of language, it is no explanation. It expands the idea that mind evolved because it is useful, and says that a key element in the evolution of mind is language, which also developed because it is useful. But just as it is empty to account for a massive advance like language simply by pointing out that speech is more useful than grunting, the same is the case with mind. A scientifically adequate account of the origin of mind would have to detail its developments, show how each occurred, and even provide evidence for stages in the development of mind as human beings evolved.

Mead does not doubt the reality of mind, and his evolutionary account – though inadequate – is an attempt to show how material body came to have mind. As a materialist he asserts we are nothing but bodies, and mind is the same as brain. But if brain and mind are identical, there remains the puzzle of what mind is made of. Mead does not believe that in the course of evolution part of body turned into spirit and that this is mind. For Mead, Freud, Rogers and Fromm, mind is real, though only the physical exists. But if mind is physical, there remains the question of how this physical brain can think, imagine, remember. Our thinking, imagining, remembering is brain activity, but at the same time it is the cause of brain activity. My deciding or remembering to take the dog for a walk is both my brain-cells reacting as well as the cause of my brain-cells reacting. How can mind both be brain and, at the same time, be independent of brain and the cause of brain reacting? Mead and other materialists fail to explain how brain functions as mind.

Granting the existence of mind – however it came about – there remains for Mead the puzzle of how human beings are free. If the two pensioners were shaped by society, how could they interpret their roles differently? If the influence of society is so powerful, if our selves are made by society, if what we are is what others expect us to be, how can each of us see the world in our own individual way? Some social behaviourists leave it there: with human personality and behaviour socially caused and determined. But Mead believes human beings to be free, and the source of that freedom is the *I*.

Mead's way out of the dead-end of determinism is by splitting the self into Me and I. It is Me that is made by what others expect; and if Me were all there was, human behaviour would be completely caused. But there is also the I. The I is the unique and spontaneous part of the self, the active agent which begins all behaviour and reacts to society inside the self, the Me. Interpreting the world differently is possible because of the I. Real human freedom exists in this interplay between I and Me. The I enables the individual to give his or her own meaning to words, gestures and other symbols. Everything begins with the unique and spontaneous I; but the I is immediately given direction by the socially made Me. The I makes possible the pensioners' unique lives and for every Hamlet to be different.

This is Mead's solution to the paradox of cause and freedom in human behaviour. There is always the Me to give direction to human behaviour but never wholly to determine it. There is always uncertainty as to how human behaviour will turn out because the I is not determined by the Me. Freedom exists because of the I.

But what does Mead add to common sense? I am free because . . . because I am I and the I is a free agent. Mead does not explain this I which rushes on stage to prevent the action of the play becoming mechanical and caused. Mead's social behaviourism rescues human behaviour from biological determinism, only to stop short of social determinism. To save human behaviour from social determinism, Mead introduces the I. As a materialist, Mead rejects any spirit in the machine, so what is the I which makes freedom possible? As it is not socially made like the Me, it must be biological; so in the end Mead returns to biology to account for human freedom. But where does this I originate? It seemed already to exist in childhood where it was playing the roles of others. Mead's account here adds little to common sense, since he resorts to the I to explain human freedom, but the I itself remains completely unexplained.

Mead believes there is a moral dimension in human beings. Being moral involves being able to adopt another's viewpoint. A slave-owner's son grows up to regard slavery as right, but coming at last to see with the eyes of a slave, he knows it is wrong. His second perspective is wider, more universal, embracing the slaves' viewpoint as well as the owners'. Moral growth is this enlarging of one's perspective to include other viewpoints. 'No man is an island . . . I am involved in Mankind'.

As the self develops, especially in childhood, it plays the roles of others and experiences their way of seeing. I can be moral only if I am acquainted with other people's viewpoints. Born into a rich Victorian household, and ignorant of the views of the poor, I adopt the perspectives of my rich parents. I can grow morally only if I become aware of other perspectives, and playing the roles of others makes this possible. Playing the roles of others, which is necessary for acquiring a self in the first place, is essential if a moral dimension is to emerge in the self. I am attracted to someone else's property, but only when I can adopt his perspective and see how he regards his property does 'Thou shalt not steal' mean anything.

Mead regards the late maturity of humans as being important for moral growth. Children's long period of dependency on adults means that the adults' point of view influences them over a long time. Language is again important, because in learning language the child becomes aware of the perspectives of others, expressed in adult speech. But it is not society alone that decides our morality – we each have our own say in the matter. At the start of a relationship with someone else's wife, a man sees the affair just from his own point of view. Later, he widens his view of the relationship to incorporate her mixed feelings, her husband's viewpoint and those of her children, her devout mother, and his own family. This enlargement of perspective to incorporate other people's viewpoints is moral growth. Moral concern and behaviour are social through and through . . . 'I am involved in Mankind'.

Moral behaviour is social even when one acts against others. A policeman sees a colleague act racially in the course of an arrest. If he adopts only the viewpoint of the racist officer, reporting him will seem anti-social. But in reporting his colleague the policeman is prompted by the viewpoint of the arrested man, the man's ethnic group and of society at large. It will be difficult for the policeman to act against his fellow officer, because the perspectives of those we interact with are a powerful influence.

Prejudice illustrates a move in the opposite direction to moral growth. In becoming prejudiced, I eliminate from my perspective the points of view of whole categories of people such as Catholics, Jews, Pakistanis ... Similarly, a society becomes more moral as its dominant viewpoint embraces the perspectives of more people: the poor, different racial and ethnic groups, the disabled, the mentally retarded, untouchables. Human beings are not born moral but become moral by extending their viewpoints to take in those of others. Mead's account of morality is interesting and insightful, but he does not explain why human beings choose to adopt points of view other than their own. Why do I – why should I – broaden my viewpoint to embrace the interests of others?

In Mead's account, human beings are not born good or bad, social or anti-social, but as blank slates that society writes on. For Freud, there is the inevitable clash between society and the individual as human biology competes with human biology to obtain gratification. For Mead, conflict is not inevitable because self and society are the result of the same social process, two sides of the same coin. The self is made by society and society is made by the self. Since the Me part of my self has developed from playing the roles of others, there can be no inherent hostility towards them. We want to be individual and separate, but we want to be part of a community; we need to be alone but we also need other people. There is no inevitable conflict between the individual and society. The I is biological, like the Freudian id, but is not dangerous. The individual and society relate in a happy dialectic, as in a good marriage. The interests of husband and wife never totally coincide, but what is good for one is good for the other in the long run.

Dangerous individuals like rapists and psychopaths do exist, but they only occur when something goes wrong and society fails to shape the self properly. Human beings are largely what other human beings make them; with good communication and interaction, those out of kilter with society can be brought back into harmony. Some changes in society may be needed if its culture is repressive, too permissive, elitist, class-ridden, racist, or unjust in other ways. But this merely means that society has failed to take into account everyone's viewpoint, and this is where the remedy lies. Nothing radical or revolutionary is needed, since the mechanisms for change which makes reform possible are present in all societies. Just as with decent management and union leaders, all that is needed for a solution to any conflict is an appreciation of the other person's viewpoint and a bit of give-and-take.

But Mead's account is rose-tinted and too optimistic. In real life there are real conflicts of interest rooted in society, and individual personalities are riven by internal struggle and guilt. Social behaviourism fails to account for this. Human beings do not take into consideration other people's viewpoints as soon as they are aware of them, especially when these compete with their own interests. The man may still continue his affair with someone else's wife even when he knows the views of all those affected. Human beings are not blank slates. Symbolic interactionism, by emphasizing the extent to which society makes people what they are, plays down the hard reality of bodily needs. The constraints of biology are real, and our genetic inheritance imposes limits on the extent to which human beings can be moulded by society.

In Freudian theory, we recognize our own emotional and passionate nature, our sexuality and aggression, but there is none of this in social behaviourism. In the social behaviourist account, human beings emerge as pale one-dimensional shadows, as actors always on stage performing, obsessed with appearances and the applause of others; there is none of the passionate concern with life's meaning that Fromm describes. In Carl Rogers' account, what we want to be is ourselves, to be fulfilled and real. For Mead, we seem concerned only with playing our roles well and conforming to obtain the approval of others. Human beings are not such bloodless phantoms, able to play any part and become any self that society wants.

Scientifically, such an account is weak. If we wished to put the social behaviourism of role theory and Mead's symbolic interactionism to the test, how would we set about it? What sort of research might be done to support such a view? And social behaviourism provides no explanation of how in fact we are shaped by the expectations of others, or even why we are. The theory relies on a common-sense assumption – of course, what other people think and expect affects us! And though how we see and interpret the world is central to Mead's view, he is not specific about the manner in which we do it. Kelly's construct theory, which we shall look at in the next chapter, does at least suggest how this is done.

But the value of the social behaviourist account remains considerable. It has made us aware how each of us is shaped by other people and of the extent to which personality is socially manufactured – in spite of the reality of biological constraints. My personality, my self and my identity seem so uniquely mine. Even when I am aware of the role of luck and circumstances in life, it still seems to me that most of what I do is by my own choice. I chose to have those sorts of friends, to act that way at school, to take that type of job, to marry that woman or man and to do this in my leisure time, believe these particular beliefs, vote X rather than Y, bring up my children in a certain way. The power of role theory and symbolic interactionism lies in making us realize that the reverse is largely true. I have not made my life the way it is because of what I am; what I am and what I do is the result of the circumstances of my life.

Symbolic interactionism helps us to see how society enters the very fabric of our being. Society creates our selves. Our selves and the choices we appear to make are not the result of biology or some God-given nature but of what society does to us. Society and culture bestow on us identity, personality, self, I, our mental health or lack of it. The social behaviourist view that we start as blank slates is not original, and is probably wrong. But social behaviourism provides an insightful perspective; it suggests that society and culture, writing on those slates, makes us human in the first place and that society and culture, writing on those slates all our lives, makes us the kind of person we are. When we realize that much of our supposedly individual lives could have been predicted by a social scientist from data such as class and the income of our parents, our lives do not appear as individual and original as we had thought. Not everyone's life and behaviour can be predicted on the basis of class, job, income and the rest – the prediction is based on probabilities. But our awareness of the overall accuracy of such prediction challenges the belief we have in the uniqueness and originality of our lives.

There are limits to the usefulness of the perspective. In Victorian society, in which middle-class women were expected to be without desire, the fact that many were highly sexed underlines the reality of biology. In Ibsen's *The Doll's House*, the husband and society combine to confirm that Nora is pretty, charming and entertaining but, since she is a woman, not to be taken seriously. Nora eventually rejects this 'feminine' self. Such personal change would be impossible – and no change in a women's personality or social role would be possible – if we were all the conformists that social behaviourism says we are. Role theory regards society as static and has difficulty in accounting for any social change and personal choice. Mead gets out of the impasse of social determinism and accounts for choice and change with the U-turn of the I; but this explains nothing. In spite of the supposed malleability of human beings, many people fail or refuse to fit in; all societies have their deviants, and totalitarian ones their dissidents. But social behaviourism rejects the idea of any underlying human nature.

Chapter Seven

THE KNOWING SCIENTISTS:
George Kelly's construct theory

> People seem not to see that their opinion of the world is also a
> confession of character.
>
> Emerson: 'Worship'

On a gravestone, below the deceased's name, is chiselled '1901–
1987, But he never made sense of it'. Men and women try to
understand the world. Like scientists they have theories and,
like scientists, they do research to test their theories. This
research is called behaviour, and what they invest in their
theories being right are their lives. This is the perspective of
personal construct theory.

Valerie is thirty, an art historian, successful but not happy in
her job, with her marriage in trouble. She goes for counselling,
and the therapist, after taking details, presents her with a pile of
blank cards. The therapist asks Valerie to write her mother's
name on one card, her father's on another, her husband's on
another, and on others the names of any brothers, sisters,
friends, close relatives. Valerie finishes with a pile of about
twenty-five cards, each naming someone important to her, and
then adds her own name. After the cards have been shuffled,
the therapist tells her to look at the first three and instructs her:
'Think of some important way in which any two of these seem
to be alike and in contrast to the third.' The cards Valerie
picks up are Father, Mother and John, a friend; pushing the
Mother and John cards to one side and the Father to the
other, she says: 'They are both intelligent, my father's a bit
stupid.' She picks up three more and separates them with
the comment: 'These two are assertive, but she's insecure.'
With the next three she says: 'They're interested in the arts

but he's not;' and with others she adopts the categories of 'intellectual/boring', 'competitive/friendly', 'rational/religious'.

Later in the day the therapist uses Kelly's same repertory grid technique with Maureen, an architect, also about thirty. She is depressed and complains of experiencing difficulty with relationships, especially with male friends. After Maureen has written down the same kinds of names, the therapist gives the same instruction. The categories Maureen adopts to divide the people on the cards are 'well-spoken/common', 'can't be trusted/reliable', 'attractive/plain', 'car-owner/does not have a car', 'left-wing/conservative', 'enterprising/lazy'.

Valerie and Maureen may or may not be saying something about the people named on the cards. In the view of construct theory they are certainly saying something about themselves. If they were asked to divide cards on a different set of people in the same way, they would adopt the same categories. Men and women develop categories to help them make sense of their lives, and with the help of these categories they see the world and other people in certain ways. Human beings are alike if they look at the world in the same way and different when they look at the world differently. 'A fool sees not the same tree that a wise man sees,' says the poet Blake.

The categories Valerie and Maureen use to describe other people express what they themselves consider important and reveal their own personalities. It is too soon for the therapist to be certain what these categories – which Kelly calls 'constructs' – reveal. But with Valerie they seem to suggest she values only people who are intelligent and intellectual, and that she is preoccupied with a competitive element in personal relations. Maureen seems concerned about externals and outward appearances and is inclined to judge people in a moralizing way.

It is not only humans who categorize the world. A hungry animal divides the world into edible and inedible, and a hunted one tries to distinguish between an escape route and a dead-end. With human beings it begins when babies divide their experience into hungry or satisfied, wet or dry, comfortable or uncomfortable. By the time they are adults humans use more complex constructs, such as Valerie's 'intelligent/stupid' and Maureen's 'well-spoken/common'. Like animals distinguishing between edible and inedible, an escape route and a dead-end, humans survive by organizing the world in this way. They use minds to do this.

Behaviourism, in the teeth of common sense, ignores mind, regarding it as irrelevant or illusory. When behaviourism became the dominant psychology between the two World Wars, mind was dismissed. By the 1950s, psychology had returned to its (common) senses and rediscovered mind, and construct theory put mind firmly back into personality. Born into a confusion of raw impressions, human beings try to make sense of things and they do it the way any animal or scientist does, by classifying experience: 'edible/inedible', 'conducts electricity/doesn't', 'wet/dry', 'assertive/insecure', 'can't be trusted/reliable'. We use constructs to impose a meaningful pattern on our experience, sometimes using new categories but usually sticking to old ones, in the end baffled by death, which refuses to fit into any. When our minds have imposed a pattern on the raw data of our experience, then we know what to think, feel and do. What we think, feel and do depends on how we see the world.

So construct theory says that to understand human beings, we need only know how they see the world. People are neither the angry infants of Freudianism, nor the rewarded pigeons of radical behaviourism, nor the players of social behaviourism. They are rational in the way common sense has always said they are; but construct theory takes this further and says they are scientists.

How do those other scientists, the officially accredited ones in white coats, set about their business? Contrary to what is popularly thought, they do not start with the data. There is no data to start with, only a confusion of raw impressions. Karl Popper has pointed out that if you ask people to 'observe', they will ask: 'What do you want us to observe?' The number of possible objects and activities one might observe is infinite, so people have to be told what to observe. Scientists, like animals after food or an escape route – or like Popper's observers – need to know what they are looking for. So scientists start with an idea of what is relevant, which is partly what a theory is. A theory – whether about the structure of particles, how cells develop, or the unconscious – gives some idea of what is relevant and what to look for. Scientists then check whether what they do find is what they expected to find; they test their predictions. 'What ought to happen if we cross these wrinkled peas with smooth ones is . . . and what we find is . . .' The rest of us carry on with our everyday lives just like this – just like scientists!

A boy wants some money; he makes an informed guess that if he helps his mother then she will give him a little something. He stays in, helps her, she pays up and confirms his theory about his mother. He may even feel that he can extend his theory to mothers in general. Behaviourists declare that the boy is only after reward but, according to construct theory, correctly predicting the way his mother would react is also important to the boy; it means the world is no longer a chaotic confusion of impressions but a place he understands. This is how grown-up scientists operate too, both the ones in white coats and the ones without them. Though their theories are more sophisticated than the boy's, the approach is the same: 'If I place this magnitude of force on copper, then . . .'; 'If I tell my wife about this other woman, then . . .'

Scientists in white coats test their predictions in a safe laboratory. But those without the white coats (the rest of us) put our theories to the test in the costly arena of life. This is what the husband is doing when he makes the prediction that he is more likely to save his marriage by confessing all to his wife. When scientists in white coats have bad theories, they do bad research. When those without white coats (like Valerie and Maureen) work with bad theories, they are unhappy, depressed, anxious, dogmatic, neurotic, and they upset their husbands or wives, boyfriends or girlfriends, or antagonize their colleagues. Our personal categories or constructs determine how we see the world and this determines how we behave. Perhaps the different constructs which Valerie and Maureen adopt do not consider all the data, ignore contradictory evidence or explain only the obvious, in the way bad theories do.

In her novel *The Waves*, Virginia Woolf uses an image to

express how each character looks at life. As a child, Susan catches a glimpse of the servants kissing; and the novelist employs this image to express how for Susan life is about passion and commitment in human relations. Her future of marriage and motherhood is decided by her way of seeing the world. For Jinny the image is the dancing leaf, the world as a delight to be enjoyed; and for Jinny everything is either pleasurable or boring. Her life is determined by this construct and becomes a search for enjoyment in society. With Rhoda, 'the tiger leaps' and 'the basin of petals' are opposites which divide the world into a terrifying reality and a safe haven. Rhoda, imprisoned in one or other alternative, eventually withdraws from life.

It is like this for all of us, because how we live is determined by how we look at life. Each of us knows the world through our own personal theories and constructs, because we use them to organize our impressions and make sense of things. Blake put it more poetically in a letter to the Reverend Dr Trusler: 'The tree which moves some to tears of joy is in the Eyes of others only a Green thing which stands in the way'. Maureen, the architect with houses to build in a dense urban area, sees the tree differently from Valerie, the keen conservationist. Maureen may find the tree beautiful but she has houses to cram in, and in general she adopts a more practical outlook on life. Each of us has a hierarchy of constructs and some are more important to us than others.

The therapist has to examine the constructs that clients use, and the repertory grid data suggests that Valerie has two main ways of looking at people. First, she regards them either as intelligent and intellectual or as stupid and boring. Secondly, she regards them as assertive and competitive or as insecure and friendly. This is the way Valerie sees people because this is the way Valerie is. Valerie values intelligent, intellectual people, and the rest of humanity she despises; and the rest of humanity – including her husband – realize this. As she treats such people with contempt, it is no wonder her marriage is in trouble. When she is with her clever colleagues at work it is different. These are the only people she can tolerate because she finds non-intellectual people boring; but she acts aggressively with them because she is competitive and regards being friendly as weakness – her second construct.

Her two dominating constructs make life miserable for Valerie. Dismissing most of humankind as stupid and boring, the only people she can mix with (apart from her husband) are intellectuals like her colleagues. But she cannot relax with them and enjoy the cut and thrust of intelligent conversation because her second construct makes her find them too threatening. Nor is this outlook any help in her marriage, since it makes her expect to win her husband's affection by impressing him with her brilliance, but it does not work.

Maureen's view of the world is different, and 'Can't be trusted/reliable', 'enterprising/lazy' suggest that Maureen looks on the world in a moralizing way. When she reads about young offenders, Maureen sees them as criminal, where others might regard them as disturbed. Where others might think they are in need of help, Maureen would have them locked away. Maureen complains about her relationships, but part of her problem is that when a friendship runs into difficulties, she blames the other people, always believing it to be their fault. As important is Maureen's obsession with externals, which limits the possibilities of male friends and friendships generally. She anticipates that only well-spoken, attractive and car-owning men will be worth spending time on. Faced with Michael and aware that he is not good-looking, Maureen sees *nothing but* the fact that he is not good-looking. Seeing him as physically unattractive, she misses the chance of enjoying Michael as someone who is knowledgeable about politics, who can give useful tips on stocks and shares, and who is witty and good company. 'Nothing-but' constructs put people in a pigeon-hole and limit the way in which we see them.

Daniel, a colleague of Valerie's, is a devout Methodist. Valerie avoids him, expecting religious people to be dogmatic, superstitious, prejudiced, reactionary. As the repertory grid revealed, Valerie divides people into either rational or religious. She then ascribes to religious people a collection of supposed characteristics, but this is *stereotyped* thinking and can make us get it wrong. This is so even when the stereotype is favourable and one regards religious people as invariably kind, considerate, and happily married.

We are most true to our scientific selves when we react to others with working hypotheses or provisional constructs. Knowing that her friend Mary is a Socialist helps Maureen make sense of her, but only so long as she realizes that there may be a great deal to Mary besides being a 'leftie'. Maureen also needs to see Mary as a keen musician, a non-practising Catholic, a single mother, and a dedicated teacher. If Maureen's 'left wing/conservative' construct is a working hypothesis used tentatively to understand Mary, it will not stereotype her. Maureen does not have to conclude from Mary's left-wing views that she is a traitor to the country or promiscuous. She does not have to conclude that because Mary is a Party member she is anti-religious; she might be, but it so happens that Mary attends Mass occasionally – which is more than many of her more conventional friends from convent school days do. Nor should the more psychologically inclined Valerie conclude, appreciating Mary's ambivalence to Catholicism, that she is an irrational neurotic working out personal problems with regard to her father. She may be, but it does not necessarily follow. One would need to explore the hypothesis, just like any scientist.

Valerie, Maureen and the rest of us are scientists trying to make sense of the world and the people round us. To do this we adopt theories, categories, constructs, hypotheses to organize the way we look at things. Construct theory has put mind firmly back into personality.

But common sense never doubted the importance of mind. Common sense always knew that values, views and beliefs are important and that they affect how we see things. What Kelly has done is to take common sense to the stimulating conclusion that we use our minds in the way scientists do, and interesting ideas follow from this. Like any scientist, we can review the theories and hypotheses that determine how we see things, and revise them if they do not work. This makes therapy possible. Therapy is not Freud's alteration of 'unbearable misery into everyday unhappiness', which can only be minimal because the unconscious is resistant to change and human behaviour is largely determined. Nor is therapy like Skinner's retraining of animals, using schedules of reinforcement. In construct theory, therapy is like scientific research, where real change is possible because we can always alter our theories in the light of experience and learn to look at the world differently. We change them in the way any self-respecting scientist does. We make predictions, check the results and if the predictions prove wrong we change the constructs and underlying theories our predictions were based on.

But like the scientists in white coats, we often have good scientific reasons for not changing our minds immediately. The behaviour of teenage children might make liberal-minded parents wonder if their tolerant style of parenthood is working, and whether they should continue with it. They may conclude that, as yet, the evidence is insufficient to justify a change. On the other hand, when change seems justified because we keep being wrong, we may fail to change because we do not realize we are wrong. Valerie continues to impress upon her husband how much cleverer she is, anticipating that this will make him love her, failing to see that it makes him angry.

Valerie, Maureen and the rest of us vary in our openness to new ideas, as official scientists do. Some, like Einstein, are able continually to re-evaluate and constantly to search for better theories. Some are so committed to old ideas that they resemble the astronomers who refused to look through Galileo's telescope. In Virginia Woolf's novel, what confronted Rhoda was not always terrifying – but she saw it as frightening, so she never advanced to test it. A prejudiced person does not abandon his prejudices just because he meets people who do not fit his stereotyped construct.

Human beings are often reluctant to change and they sometimes find change difficult. Neurotics, and people like Valerie and Maureen, have particular difficulty, like bad scientists sticking to theories long after they have proved useless and should have been abandoned. This is why they are anxious, unhappy and depressed, and have problems at work, in their relationships, their marriages and with their friends.

But construct theory does not doubt that change can and does occur. How is this possible? Is it free will? Driving home at night, a woman realizes that her car bonnet has struck something – or someone. She knows she could be in trouble, especially as she has had a few drinks, and she drives on. Further on, thinking of her own children safe at home, she reflects that it might be someone else's child she has hit and left lying in the road. Seeing the situation differently, she stops and drives back. Kelly believes that men and women are free. Their freedom consists in being able to see things differently; and when they do, they act differently.

But freedom is never total. Though we see a situation first one way then choose to see it another way and change, usually we can choose only from the constructs we already have. Free choice is made possible by our constructs but is limited by them. An employer regards his workers as lazy and as a result is tough with them; later he changes to seeing them as hard-working if treated well and consequently he treats them better. He has shifted from one end of a 'lazy/hardworking' construct to the other, but he has not abandoned the construct altogether and seen them as 'exploited'. The employees are just there and may be regarded in any way at all: as poorly trained, militant, easy-going, scared of working themselves out of a job, stirred up by trouble-makers, badly supervised. The choice of how the employer regards them, his freedom, and the limits on his choice are the result of his personal construct system.

But though freedom is not total, even our constructs can change. A young man sees his father at one moment as a tyrant to be obeyed, and at another as a bully to rebel against. But in the course of life or therapy, he may come to see him as a frightened, lonely man to be forgiven and loved.

For Kelly, freedom and determinism are two sides of the same coin and there is no problem in reconciling them. Human behaviour is determined since, once I see the world in a certain way, what I do inevitably follows. But I am free in the first place to see the world how I will. A young woman, having an affair with a friend's husband, regards it as the best thing that ever happened to her. Later, seeing it as likely to cause pain all around, she brings the affair to an end. For Freud, human beings are trapped by their biology and childhood. For Skinner and the behaviourists, they are trapped by their schedules of reinforcement. For social behaviourists, they are actors trapped in the roles they are playing. According to Kelly, humans are no more trapped by their constructs than are scientists by their theories; they can always change them.

Human beings can always change their point of view and look at things differently. What they cannot do is abandon all viewpoints. No scientist, with or without a white coat, can live and work in this way. We all need a theory about the world to operate with and constructs to organize our experience. If I am throwing a party and some of the young people coming have an Afro-Caribbean background, it would make sense to get hold of records for dancing, and not waltzes and quicksteps. It may sound attractive to approach the world and other people with a completely open mind, but the result would be chaos.

The human scientist, like the one in a white coat, must have some framework with which to consider even a party. Without the framework, the party would be chaotic because I could not anticipate what sort of records were needed or even if music were needed at all. The anticipation and control that a theory or construct provides is always necessary, though sometimes they need to be tentative. I do not have to over-control and put on a reggae record immediately the young black students arrive and usher them on to the dance floor; this might lead to their becoming bored, since what they really wanted was intelligent conversation in a quiet corner. However, with no framework at all to plan, the party would be chaos. If there is a lot to drink and loud music it would be embarrassing and hurtful if – to show my open-mindedness – I had invited the strictly teetotal Brethren from next door. Human beings are knowing scientists; they apply theories and constructs in order to make sense of their lives and try to achieve a balance between too little and too much control, between chaos and boredom.

But stimulating though Kelly's ideas are, he has not solved the problem of free will. What Kelly has done is to move freedom from the point where we act to where we see and interpret the situation. He has merely described human freedom differently, by saying we are free because we can change the way we see things. But how do we change the way we see things? How, in a universe where everything proceeds by cause and effect, can we *choose* the way in which we see a situation? What is it that enables us to abandon one viewpoint and adopt another? An atheist takes up religious belief and a believer chooses to abandon his faith. A young Austrian is conscripted into military service; his family and friends and his priest tell him he has no alternative but to go. He chooses to see it differently – war is wrong, this war is wrong – and he goes before the firing squad instead. With human beings, freedom relates to how we can choose the way we see a situation, says Kelly; our behaviour follows inevitably from how we see things. This is a stimulating idea, but it fails to solve the problem of free will, since it never explains how in fact we are free to choose or to change the way we see a situation.

There is another difficulty with Kelly's account of free choice. The woman described earlier may – in some unexplained way – come to see her love affair differently and regard it as wrong. But she still may not end it. I once regarded smoking as macho, so I smoked. I now see it differently, as anti-social, as giving me bad breath and cancer so I . . . stop smoking? I may or may not manage it.

In construct theory, personal relations are not a Freudian marketplace exchange, nor Skinnerian mutual reinforcement. They are about understanding other people, anticipating how they will behave, and reacting appropriately. A good theory or set of constructs makes this possible. But a good theory or set of constructs is just what a neurotic lacks. The last time the husband was unfaithful he told his wife everything, and it should have been obvious she would have preferred not to have known. In spite of this, this time he intends to tell her everything again.

But the husband, Valerie and Maureen do not have to stick to their old theories, since all theories can be revised or scrapped and better ones put in their place. In therapy and life there is always the opportunity to adopt alternative constructs when the ones we have do not work. If Valerie can stop believing that the only important thing is to be clever, she will stop contemptuously dismissing the rest of humanity as beneath her. The rest of humanity, including her husband, will react to her changed views, and her life will become richer. If she stopped regarding it as weak and insecure to be friendly, she would cease to see her colleagues as threatening and would enjoy their company. There is no true and correct way to look at the world and other people, but some ways are more useful than others. I can regard the people I work with as congenial companions with interesting ideas or as plain-clothes detectives paid by an enemy to spy on me, deceiving me with their smiles.

At eighteen Joseph has an affair with a married woman whom he meets through a politically active friend. For Joseph this is a great erotic experience, the sexual liberation he has been longing for. The affair ends and they go their separate ways – but not quite. In between the love-making she had introduced him to the writings of Karl Marx, and after the parting he continues to read with ever-increasing interest and belief. He begins to look back on the affair as a fortuitous introduction to the real liberation, the political one of Marxism, and in retrospect the sex seems less important. After a few years, now disillusioned with radical politics and turned on to individual psychology and Freud, he sees his adolescent affair with an older woman as the acting out of an unresolved oedipus complex. Years later, now middle-aged and a born-again Christian, he remembers with guilt and shame his youthful adultery. Which version of Joseph's teenage affair is most useful, and which one is true?

Though other theories claim to state what is true and really going on, for construct theory there is no single, true account. For the Freudian, the affair really was a re-enactment of Joseph's childhood oedipal relations with his parents – this is the correct account. Freudian psycho-analysis addresses Joseph: 'You may physically have been in the arms of this other woman but in phantasy you were really sleeping with your mother. When you come here and talk about your wife and what happened last week, it is really what happened years ago with your mother you are telling me about.' Construct theory – which is criticized for being too much a 'general theory' – makes no such attempt to suggest a specific version, but says that the relevant account is the individual's own. According to construct theory, the individual's own account reveals more than any other version, even if this other version is Freud's, Fromm's or that of some other famous theorist. It is Joseph's account we are interested in, since it is Joseph's account which reveals his personality. As Blake said: 'As a man is, so he sees'.

But in suggesting that we can understand someone's personality from their account of reality, construct theory is implying that everyone's reality, expressed in their construct system, is unique and private. This may present no problem when someone's construct is of the 'car-owner/does not have a car' or 'left-wing/conservative' public variety. But how can private constructs, such as Valerie's 'intellectual/boring', 'competitive/friendly', or even Maureen's 'enterprising/lazy', be fully understood by anyone else? According to construct theory, in order to understand other people one has to get inside their mind by finding out their personal constructs. But certain personal constructs are such that another person can never find out what they really mean to the individual. The contents of another's mind will always remain essentially private and be understood only by the person whose mind it is. If this is the case, how can I or the therapist know what Valerie means by 'assertive/insecure' or Maureen by 'enterprising/lazy'? So why attempt to understand others in terms of their individual, subjective and private experience when the enterprise is doomed to failure? Why not adopt the approach of true science and explain human personality and behaviour in terms of public and objective data, in the way behaviourism and psycho-analysis do?

However, the criticism, that it is too much a general theory, refers also to construct theory's abstract nature and lack of empirical content. The charge is that Kelly's perspective provides a useful framework within which to consider people, but nothing more. Do boys have sexual feelings for their mothers? Is our behaviour affected by reward? Do we have a drive to fulfil our potential? Construct theory says nothing on these lines because it does not address specific questions. Where other theories propose that human beings are angry babies, intelligent pigeons or actors, construct theory merely says that what people are depends on how they choose to see the world. How people act and react depends on the theories and constructs they adopt in order to make sense of the world; and since this is how scientists operate, construct theory concludes we might usefully call them scientists. However, the theory does at least go on to provide, particularly with the repertory grid technique, a way of finding out what constructs individual people have of the world.

Construct theory extends this very general approach to moral questions. There may be good and bad as objective values out there in the world, but Kelly is interested in good and bad, right and wrong, only as categories in people's minds: 'There is nothing either good or bad, but thinking makes it so'. Whether I see sex before marriage as harmless, as wrong or as good experience depends on my constructs. It is my constructs that Kelly's psychology concerns itself with. The theory and the grid technique provide a means of investigating the moral constructs that people have and how they acquire and develop them. But the theory says nothing of what *really* is right and wrong, and whether there *really* is a moral element in humans which distinguishes between good and bad. Kelly's theory is not interested in these questions since it is a psychological theory, not an ethical one.

Similarly, construct theory passes no opinion on whether people are inclined to good or evil or are just blank slates. The only sense in which they are morally anything is when they adopt moral labels to describe themselves and others. If I describe myself as evil and my mother as good, this is of interest to the therapist. But these 'moral' labels are only psychological statements revealing something about myself. 'Psycho-analysis defines guilt in terms of the moral turpitude of accomplishing or seeking to accomplish injury to someone,' says Kelly. 'Personal construct psychology leaves the matter of moral turpitude *per se* to systems other than psychological.' Construct theory does not state whether humans have a moral nature or if they are good or bad; it does not regard it the business of a general psychological theory to do so.

A more specific criticism of construct theory is its individualism. Both Fromm and the social behaviourism of role theory and Mead state that society and culture shape our personalities. Kelly says very little about how our constructs are formed and the part society and culture may play in this. Significantly, he writes very little on children since this would involve having to say something about the development of constructs. Research could certainly be carried out within the framework of construct theory to discover how constructs originate in childhood and develop in the maturing individual. But the theory's interest is not in our past; construct theory is concerned with the here and now, and with our capacity to change in the here and now.

Where in construct theory, with its emphasis on mind, do feelings fit in? In Kelly's scientist we recognize the rational human being, but where is the Freudian creature of emotion we also see in ourselves? Sitting in his bath, it occurred to Archimedes how the weight of a solid related to the water it displaced. His cry of '*Eureka*' (translated as 'I've got it') conveys the thrill of seeing something new. Archimedes' excitement illustrates that feeling and reason are not separate but one.

Kelly disliked the split in theories of personality between feeling and reason, between emotion and intellect, just as T. S. Eliot did in literature. When a man sees a woman in an exciting and new way, he experiences the thrill of falling in love. Valerie, realizing for the first time that her husband no longer wants to live with her, is intensely sad. Maureen believes her father is alive, but a day later when the news arrives she has to reclassify him as dead and she feels grief. Emotion and feeling relate to change and seeing things differently. We base our lives on how we see the world, and if how we see the world changes significantly we will feel emotion. A woman has a 'born again' religious conversion and replaces her old secular outlook with a view of the universe as an arena of sin, grace and redemption. She will feel great emotion, just as she would if – with a loss of faith – the change were in the opposite direction.

We all of us, as scientists, invest a great deal in our views of the world. Our personal experience may (to our satisfaction) confirm our views or may show that they are wrong. If a current view is shown to be wrong but at the same time we see a better one, we get excited. Falling in love or the act of conversion are just such enlarged, more satisfying views. But with so much of our lives invested we feel emotion when we exchange one view for another, whether it be conversion, falling in love or loss of faith. We also react with feeling when our views are under threat – witness the hostility of the astronomers who refused to look through Galileo's telescope. Human society has grasped how disturbing it is to change the way we see things. Culture has developed rites of passage to assist in certain changes in life such as adolescence, the loss of a loved one in death, or the change from being single to marriage and parenthood. But any change in the way we see the world, whether passing an exam or being deserted by one's husband or wife, is an occasion of strong feeling. A human being is one unified whole, and there is no separation of emotion and intellect. Feelings are about changes in the way we see the world and people and ourselves.

Any theory of personality, however, inevitably emphasizes some areas at the expense of others. The stuff of raw emotion and conflict which fills the daily papers, the divorce courts and Freud is less in evidence in construct theory. Kelly's account of human beings as scientists stresses our reason and thought at the expense of placing less emphasis on emotion.

What is Kelly's account of mind and how it relates to body? We may observe Maureen in two horizontal positions, first on the operating table, secondly on the psychotherapist's couch. Scalpel in hand the surgeon sees the anaesthetized Maureen, with a nasty growth on her knee, as body. The surgeon does not concern himself with Maureen's anxieties, loves, hates and boyfriend problems. The psychotherapist, faced with Maureen recumbent but wide awake on the couch, concentrates on just such anxieties, loves, hates and difficulties with men. An important view of Maureen and people in general is the surgeon's – as body. A second important view is the therapist's – as mind. Body and mind are in the eye of the beholder, and Maureen is neither body nor mind, but a person.

Body and mind – the surgeon's perspective and the therapist's – are two important ways of looking at human beings. Kelly is no dualist and there are not two things, body and mind, but one thing, a person. Body and mind are different perspectives on a person. What matters more for Kelly is mind – the psychotherapist's perspective, not the surgeon's – because only this is relevant to his account of personality. As a result, construct theory need not bother with the body–mind problem which – for Kelly – is merely about two different ways of seeing a person. Kelly avoids having to address the body–mind problem by regarding it as irrelevant to his theory.

But body and mind are only two of the many ways of looking at Maureen. She can be looked at in terms of her biochemistry, social class, religion, economic situation, her interests . . . The list of possible perspectives is almost endless, and not one of them is definitive. There is never going to be a single correct version of what Maureen is, nor a final reckoning when we *really* have a definitive account of human personality. This is Kelly's philosophical position which he calls constructive alternativism. This view, which underlies construct theory, says that there is no one truth, only a variety of possible views of the world and personality.

Kelly dispenses with the unconscious of Freudian theory, though his psychology can cope with the unconscious by talking of constructs out of awareness. We may have personal constructs which affect our behaviour but which we are not aware of because they originated when we were babies and without language. But again, emphasizing one aspect of personality is done only at the expense of another. In choosing to see humans as conscious and rational, Kelly minimizes the role of any unconscious.

The knowing scientist of construct psychology does not possess a mind looking out on and categorizing the world. This categorizing mind looking out on the world and putting it into constructs *is* the human scientist. And the human scientist's use of constructs (modifying and abandoning some, adopting others) suggests a capacity for self-awareness that we associate with consciousness. But mind, the person, consciousness, are all assumed by construct theory, and Kelly makes no attempt to explain them. Nor does he try to account for how they originate, in the way Mead does. Construct psychology simply assumes what common sense tells us: we are mind-full, self-aware and conscious creatures.

Kelly extends the importance of conscious and active mind in personality to suggest that people are like scientists – indeed, *are* scientists. With this thought-provoking idea he provides an insightful perspective. The idea that people are scientists, trying to make sense of the world and their lives, puts mind and cognitive processes back at the centre of personality and returns to a traditional view of men and women as rational beings. Mind, and not instinct or reinforcement, is what personality is about. Each of us sees the world in the way we do because of what is important to us. So the categories in which we choose to see the world become a confession of character. I see people as intelligent or stupid, competitive or friendly, because this is what is important for me. Each of us is different because we see the world differently, and we behave differently because we have different views of the world to test out. Some of our views are useful and work, and this leads to normal and healthy behaviour. Other views do not work or they work less well, and we have neurotic behaviour. The insights that emerge from construct theory are useful in themselves, but they also provide a new perspective for therapy. If we cannot cope with life it is because we are working with inadequate theories and constructs; in this case what we need to do – in therapy and in life – is to replace them with better ones, ones that fit the facts better.

For Kelly there are many possible accounts of reality, and a variety of possible accounts of personality itself, some better than others. Such a view enables construct theory to be eclectic and to incorporate ideas and insights from psycho-analysis, behaviourism and other perspectives.

But there are limits to the philosophical position of construct theory, that the world out there is what I say it is. My conscious mind may categorize the approaching sports car as a consumer durable, as a fine piece of design or as a phallic symbol; but this will not prevent it also being mass with velocity which ends my consciousness when we collide. The world has a reality independent of that which is pictured in my mind. Construct theory does not explain personality; but Kelly, by inverting Blake's words to suggest that 'As a man sees, so he is', proposes that human beings are usefully to be regarded as a sort of scientist. This makes us aware of how central mind is to personality, but common sense had never doubted the importance of mind.

Chapter Eight

THE MYSTERY

There is always something irrational to be added, something that simply cannot be explained, a *deus ex machina* or asylum of ignorance, that well-known nickname for God.

Jung: *The Development of Personality*

Arthur C. Clarke's *2001* ends with the astronaut up to his neck in difficulties. 'Then he waited, marshalling his thoughts and brooding over his still untested powers. For though he was master of the world, he was not quite sure what to do next. But he would think of something.' The impudence of 'But he would think of something' is at first seductive, but eventually one becomes aware of the arrogance. 'Don't worry,' the sentence is saying, 'human beings will find a solution – they always do.'

The human species has certainly survived so far, but at what a cost – of individuals, groups and societies! Famine, war, slavery, concentration camps, holocausts are no evidence of any human talent for finding solutions, 'final' or otherwise. Influenced by false ideas of science, we think that all problems have solutions and that, like Arthur C. Clarke's astronaut, the human species will always 'think of something'.

In this no-nonsense approach, personality is just another problem about to be solved. If the zoologist's naked ape explanation fails, the computer account will come up with something. If this also fails, there is always another solution rising above the horizon. Scientists may soon have a complete description of how the brain works. When this happens, goes the no-nonsense view, we will discard id, self, constructs, roles, relationships, rewards, for an explanation of mind and personality in terms of brain-cells and chemistry. It is materialism on promise, but the possibility does exist that naked ape, computer, brain-cell accounts (or whatever follows) will succeed where others have failed.

Or they may fail, like the rest. Human personality may not be another problem about to be solved. It certainly seems unlikely to be explained by comparison with any animal, with reference to any machine, or in terms of brain-cells and chemistry. It is difficult to see why any comparison with animals should explain human personality. Human beings differ from other animals in language, consciousness, culture and creativity, and in many other ways. Even if such differences were merely of degree, the degree of difference is large enough to cast doubt on any explanation of human beings that is based on chimpanzees or other apes. Humans have so many features specific to humans. There seems no point in explaining personality in terms of apes, creatures without culture or language, without much in the way of consciousness and creativity, and which do not usually kill their own kind.

With computer explanations of personality, there is the added limitation that computers are not alive. Even the most ardent advocates of artificial intelligence have yet to claim that in the computer they have created a machine like Frankenstein's monster, that lives and breathes. The emergence of life changes everything – it certainly transforms matter and it means that living beings are not just the sum of their material parts. Human beings are more than the water and minerals that constitute them, and human personality is more than the mechanisms the computer attempts to simulate.

With brain research there remains the difficulty of our subjective experience. The reality of the person on the receiving end of experience cannot be reduced to brain-cells and chemistry. *I* feel pain and hope and believe and love and remember. Personal, subjective experience has not yet been accounted for, and it is difficult to know how it could be by any advance in brain research. An objective description in terms of brain-cells and chemistry cannot explain (or explain away) what can be known only in the first person – my experience, as I feel pain and hope and believe and love and remember. As yet, the experience of being human cannot even be captured other than by poets, novelists and dramatists; it certainly cannot be described scientifically.

Theories of personality present us with a variety of perspectives. Freud's angry, sexual baby, adult on the outside, infant inside, forever reliving childhood, a danger to itself and others ... Skinner's mindless organism, like a clever pigeon, its behaviour mere habit, shaped by reward and punishment ... Rogers' flower people, seeking to be human, to live fulfilled lives, twisted from their nature by love with strings attached ... Fromm's caring liberals, free but lonely, in a Godless universe, isolated by capitalism, looking to find meaning in life through love, solidarity, work ... Social behaviourism's actors, playing life's roles, acting with such conviction that they convince themselves, forget they are only acting and become the parts they are playing ... Kelly's applied scientists, the world their laboratory, their behaviour their research, trying to make sense of the data of their lives ...

Confronted by these views, none obviously nonsense, our reaction may well be one of wonder, like Miranda's. We could have added others: Cattell's factor and Allport's trait approaches, Eysenck's biological account, Jung's analytical psychology, the neo-Freudianism of Klein and Erikson, Adler's individual psychology, the object relations school of Fairbairn. If our six theories complemented each other, we would simply be puzzled by how many-faceted and multidimensional personality is. But at times the theories scarcely appear to be describing the same human animal, and at other times they plainly contradict one another.

According to one account, human mind is illusion. According to another, mind is real but people begin as bodies and mind develops later. Other accounts do not attempt to explain how mind develops, assuming that it exists at birth. On another view, mind and consciousness are ways of describing people, merely adjectives; only people are real. Or mind is real, and its important part is conscious ... or the important part of mind is unconscious. The different perspectives confront one another, leave much unexplained, and sometimes contradict common sense.

Common sense is a knowledge of obvious truths. Much of the common-sense view we have of personality originates from our experience of being human. Common sense, informed and enlightened by the growth of science, is in part a developing body of knowledge. But only in part. When a theory of personality announces in the name of science that mind does not exist, common sense knows this is nonsense. From our experience we know the difference between being awake, thinking, reflecting, remembering, and being unconscious, under anaesthetic, blind drunk; it is the difference mind makes.

Sitting in the sun, I think how hot it is, remember yesterday and reflect I was hotter then. A dog may think how hot it is, though a dog does little enough thinking. The dog certainly does not reflect how much hotter it felt yesterday. The human mind has a self-awareness that other animals lack, and this we call consciousness. Consciousness is an awareness of my thoughts, memories, reflections. My consciousness is ... I. I think, I remember, I reflect, and there is no breaking down 'I' into parts and explaining it. 'I' is not the product of experience because without 'I' there would be no experience. 'I' exists and does things and usually does them for a reason.

Common sense does not know what 'I' is but it knows that there is an 'I' in every human being. Common sense suspects that to exist like a snail, without any conscious I, is like hardly existing at all. Human beings have consciousness; other animals have very little; computers have none. 'Every time a man dies, a whole universe is destroyed' (Popper-Lynkeus). It is the end of human consciousness at someone's death which makes us sad; no one grieves at the 'death' of a computer. And common sense knows this conscious I interacts with body: I see that the lights are green and put my foot on the accelerator; my body has a virus infection which makes me feel depressed. But common sense does not know how body and mind interact.

The six theories present diverging views on freedom as well as on mind. Our behaviour is not free but caused since everything in nature is caused, and we are part of nature. According to another view, when the conflicting pressures upon us are balanced, we are free to choose, but only from available alter-

natives. Or most of the time we are not free because of unconscious forces; when these forces become conscious we are free.
Or we are free because of the 'I' each one of us is. Or what we
do is determined by the way we see things, but we are free to
choose the way we see things. Or human actions are caused by
our bodies. Human actions are caused not by our bodies but by
rewards and punishments. Human actions are the product of
our past history. It is the pressures of society and culture in the
present that determine what we do ... The different theories
contradict one another, fail to solve the problem of free will and
determinism, and some contradict common sense.

Common sense says that sometimes humans are free, make
choices and could have acted differently. A middle-aged man
may be pushed or pulled by his body in the direction of a
younger woman, but his body does not decide his behaviour –
he does. If he goes off with a younger woman he could probably
have acted differently and his wife would be right to take it
personally. If there is no free will, then no one is responsible,
and no one should be praised or blamed. If free will does not
exist, then we should never feel guilty, or need to.

But with the growth of scientific knowledge, common sense
has enough sense to realize that we are not completely free and
that sometimes we are not free at all. Our bodies, past experience
and history, and the pressure of present circumstances shape
our behaviour and sometimes even determine what we do. How
this freedom of mine interacts with my body, with past history
and present circumstances, common sense does not know. It is
not easy in any situation to know where cause ends and where
freedom and responsibility begin. That, as they say, is for the
courts to decide. But getting up in the night to close the gate,
instead of ignoring it and going back to sleep, is different from
the wind blowing the gate open in the first place. 'We know our
wills are free, and there's an end on't,' said Dr Johnson. What
informed and enlightened common sense asserts is that some of
the time we are free and that we are more free at some times
than at others.

Our six theories also present a variety of positions on the
moral ideas of good and bad, right and wrong. There is the view

that good is what gives pleasure. There is the view that good is what is psychologically healthy. There is the view that good is what has desirable consequences for society. Bad is the opposite of these. There is also the view that ideas of good, bad, right and wrong are ethical issues and irrelevant to psychology. Our six theories differ, seem not to explain morality satisfactorily, and sometimes contradict common sense.

One view, that of Carl Rogers, does adopt the common-sense perspective, which is usually also that of religion. According to this view good and bad, right and wrong really do exist, are in human nature and are universal. What appear to be moral differences in different societies are usually only on the surface. In one culture elderly parents are placed by their children in nice old people's homes. In some nomadic cultures the elderly are left to die by a river they cannot cross. What the elderly want least in a nomadic society is to become a threat to the survival of the tribe. When there is no alternative but for them to die by a river they cannot cross, the children reluctantly leave them, because this is what their parents want. In both cultures the young are trying to do what is best for their parents.

This common-sense view holds that what is right and wrong will be found to be much the same in different cultures. Betraying other people's trust, rape and murder are considered wrong in most – if not all – societies. Where there appear to be differences we find that if we look below the surface – as with the nomads – this is usually not the case. In all societies the young are expected to honour and care for their parents. Young people may not always do so but this is because they have free will. Nothing makes slavery, torture or a holocaust anything other than evil. So when a theory announces in the name of science that moral laws are like the rules of the game of marbles, just something to be agreed, or are merely herd instinct, common sense knows that this is nonsense.

If common sense is wrong, then what separates Gandhi, Martin Luther King or Mother Teresa from Hitler and Stalin is only bad training, different temperaments, fortunate and unfortunate circumstances, or being mentally ill. Science has made us aware how inborn temperament, present circumstances and our past (especially our childhood) shape our behaviour. But common sense knows that they do not always determine what we do, and that right and wrong partly remain a matter of choice. Common sense asserts that human beings have an inner voice telling them what is right and wrong. Human beings try to live by this voice, some trying harder than others, and everyone often fails, which is why we feel guilt. Walking across a bridge, I see a woman jump into a river but do nothing. Years later I feel – as I did at the time – I ought to have done something. Even if there were a herd instinct which said, 'Save her,' and an instinct for self-preservation which said, 'Don't risk your skin,' there remained a third voice which told me which of the other two I *ought* to obey. This third voice, which common sense calls conscience, is real – though common sense does not know what it is.

When it comes to the Jekyll and Hyde question, personality theories again provide a variety of perspectives. In one account humans are so driven by self-interest, so touched by a primitive hostility to others, that society has to crush them. In another account people are good, and any bad they do is because the sick societies they inhabit frustrate their need to live fulfilled lives. According to another view humans are good, their natures distorted only by the strings-attached love of their parents. Or humans are blank slates, neither good nor bad, simply what reward and punishment make them. Or, since good and bad and morality are a fiction, there exist only people's needs in competition and society intervening to control the conflict. Or there is no inevitable conflict between the individual and others. Self and society are two sides of the same coin, and their interests coincide. Or again, this moral dimension is irrelevant to psychology except as a category which people use to classify others.

Common sense remains puzzled by the Jekyll and Hyde question and cannot decide whether human beings are good, bad, indifferent, or just blank slates. But there is already a serpent in paradise; born into a world where evil exists, we immediately feel its influence. Good and bad, common sense suggests, are something to do with people's nature, their experience and the situation, but also to do with free choice. But common sense has enough sense to realize that this is no explanation.

Our six theories sometimes contradict common sense, and sometimes – as with the idea of an unconscious – they supplement common sense; sometimes common sense supplements them. Freud does not really explain mind or ego, but he can assume that we know what he is getting at because of our everyday experience of mind and I. Freud does not explain how mind relates to body, but he can assume that we know it does. Human beings are not really like the plumbing – which is what we are like, according to Freud's instinct theory. But because the theory can rely on our knowledge of what it is like to be human, Freud's idea of instincts partly succeeds because we can clothe it with our common-sense experience. In his personality theory Freud refers to tension and tension reduction and cathectic discharge, but when it comes to psycho-analytic therapy it is common-sense notions of love, loss and grief that are used to help people.

Skinner's perspective causes double vision. We cannot but be impressed by the originality of his account of human beings in terms of rewards and punishments. But Skinner's creation of such a theory, and our understanding of it, assumes mind-full and insight-full intelligence of a sort which would not be possible if his theory were right. The self is central to Rogers, and central to the self is the I; but Rogers gives no adequate explanation of this active I. The theory can work only by assuming our common-sense knowledge of the I and how it operates. The same is true of the self in Mead's social behaviourism. Also important in Rogers is a master motive, a desire to live fulfilled lives. But this is not explained or accounted for, though we may know what he means from our personal experience.

Fromm's human being is very human, and we recognize the men and women he describes as they love and work and care and try to find meaning in their lives. But Fromm is appealing to our common knowledge and shared experience, whereas he is supposed to be explaining them. He rarely mentions mind, though mind is assumed in his account. In Mead's social behaviourism, freedom is possible because each of us is capable of interpreting the world uniquely. What makes this possible is the I of common sense, but Mead fails to account for this I. Where body fits into Mead's picture also remains unclear, but this too is left to common sense. Construct theory assumes the workings of conscious mind which it never explains; but the theory works because Kelly can appeal to our everyday appreciation of what he means. We are free because we can see things in a variety of ways, says Kelly, but what that freedom is which enables us to see things in a variety of ways is not explained but assumed.

Theories of personality would falter and fail without this unrecognized recourse to common sense. 'She cried because she was sad at the death of her father' ... 'She bought tickets for the show because they both liked musicals and she wanted to take her husband somewhere for his birthday' ... 'He married her for her money' ... Much of what we do is adequately described by common sense; personality psychology supplements common sense and only rarely supplants it. Scientific theories of personality would frequently have little meaning without an unadmitted appeal to common sense.

More sophisticated accounts and new ways of thinking about people continue to emerge and develop in psychology. Occasionally they inform and shape common sense. It is possible that eventually we will arrive at a grand theory, or at a combination of those we already have, and the problem of personality will be solved. What seems more likely is that scientific accounts will leave personality unexplained. Personality is a puzzle, not because of the shortcomings of present theories, soon to be remedied by bigger and better ones, but because of the nature of what we are studying. We end up with a kaleidoscope of one-dimensional perspectives because of the nature of personality. Personality will probably always remain a puzzle behind the perspectives of different theories, even when they are supplemented by an informed and enlightened common sense. However good the theory or combination of theories, we will always be left with a sense of something crucial having slipped through our fingers.

The real difficulty lies in not being able to step back and consider personality objectively. It is not possible to make personality into an object of detached scientific inquiry since it is not something that each of us has. Personality is something each of us is. I can never stand back from my personality and examine it from the outside, in the way I can examine the chair I sit on. It is not that I am a little too close but that I am much too close and am part of the thing itself. The French philosopher Gabriel Marcel distinguished between a problem and a mystery. Personality is not a problem to be solved, like building a bridge, because it is not a problem at all. It is, in Marcel's terms, a mystery.

How I build a bridge or solve an equation are problems because I am outside them. I stand apart from the materials for the bridge and the building plans. There is a separation between the bridge to be built and the builder, just as there is a separation between the equations and the mathematician who will solve them. The separation or distinction is between object and subject. But when we study mind, the subject–object distinction does not exist. I cannot stand apart from mind and examine it from the outside because, whatever mind is, it is something that I am. For this reason, mind – in Marcel's terms – is a mystery, and complete explanations are not possible with mysteries.

A woman whose marriage is in trouble says to the counsellor: 'My husband needs a mother as well as a wife. I understand that, but he's leaning on me and pretending he's in charge. When our son was born, all my husband's oedipal feelings came to a head and I responded hostilely.' The wife is standing outside the relationship and talking about it in a way a mechanic would talk about faults in a car. Modern science regards everything as an object which the scientist investigates from the outside. Scientists look at what they investigate as (in Marcel's sense) a problem, and this is what the wife is doing. She is seeing the relationship with her husband as a problem she is separate from. Her account may well provide intellectual insight, but in a relationship one can never stand completely outside the experience of the other person.

A psychologist, especially if influenced by behaviourism,

might see this couple's problems as sexual and would train them in better techniques of intercourse. Problems have solutions which have only to be found and, like Arthur C. Clarke's astronaut, we will always think of something. Techniques, like training in improved methods of intercourse, might be part of the solution. There is much to commend this no-nonsense approach since most tasks – such as building a house or designing an electronic system – are like this. It may even be useful to regard many human difficulties as problems, though usually they are more than just problems. It might help the wife to analyse the marriage in her intellectual way with the counsellor, or for the psychologist to train the woman and her husband in better sexual technique. But if one of the partners (or both) is unwilling to be committed to the relationship, no amount of talking or improved orgasms will save the marriage. Commitment, love, relationships are mysteries, not objects we can stand apart from and investigate from the outside.

A psychologist gives a battery of aptitude and interest tests to a married woman seeking careers guidance on returning to work. Looking at her scores on the tests the psychologist knows a lot *about* her and, after a detached professional interview, is in a position to advise on jobs. The psychologist may know more *about* aspects of her personality than the man who has lived with her for twenty years and who loves her. But the husband knows her better, as opposed to knowing *about* her, than the detached professional with test scores and interview data. For the psychologist, she becomes a career problem for which there exists a solution; but for the husband who loves her, she remains a person and a mystery.

The detached, objective psychologist records her aptitude and interest scores and notes her performance in interview but misses the person. Reducing the woman to parts, to test scores and interview information may solve her career problem, but does not enable the psychologist to know her in the way her husband does. Such is our regard for science, however, that we believe the psychologist, zoologist and computer buff with their objective techniques understand the woman better than her husband. Between the husband and the woman he loves there is not the clear separation that exists between the psychologist and the woman or between the mechanic and a car. But her husband knows her in the only way mysteries can be known: through experience. As soon as we stand outside someone with the objectivity of science, like the psychologist advising the woman on careers, we miss the experience. If – like the husband – we stay with the experience, the objectivity of science is not possible.

Seeing personality as a problem has produced valuable insight and knowledge. We have outlined only a fraction of the information provided by three traditions in psychology – the psycho-analytic, behaviourist and humanist. However helpful and revealing such accounts are, they fail to explain personality, and they always will. Every human personality is a mystery, and the best one can do with a mystery is to experience it. The father's tongue-in-cheek advice to his son, 'Don't try to understand women, just love them,' makes this point. A man who loves a woman may not know much *about* her as a brilliant lecturer or an anxiety neurotic, and a woman who loves a man may not know much *about* him as a promising engineer or as an educational under-achiever; but each can still know the other deeply as a person. The man and woman could, of course, both know *about* the other intellectually as a problem to be understood and know the other as a mystery to be experienced. But full understanding, possible with a problem, is not possible with a mystery.

This becomes clear when we break personality down into parts. Whatever the 'I' is, it is not something I have which can be considered from the outside. Whatever 'I' is, it is something I am. If Freud's ego is an attempt to give an objective account of the I, it inevitably fails because the I is not something I can give an objective account of. I cannot stand apart and examine the I or ego from the outside since it is the I or ego that stands apart and examines. As soon as I stand outside the I, it becomes the Me. This is what happens in Mead and in Rogers and makes their I and self into the Me of common sense. With construct theory we cannot get outside the construing person we are and construe ourselves, since each of us is the construing person. Skinner, abandoning common sense totally and ignoring all human experience, regards the I as an illusion, leaving us puzzled as to what actually does the regarding. If we stay with common sense and regard mind and I as real, there is no way in which we can know them objectively. Mind and I are not unsolved problems awaiting a solution but mysteries for which no scientific explanation is possible. 'How can the knower be known?'

The same is true for the question of how body and mind relate. Philosophers have considered the body–mind problem for hundreds of years, but all that has been achieved is its narrowing down in recent times to a brain–mind problem. In theories such as Mead's, it is difficult to see where body or brain fit into so social and non-biological an account of personality. Kelly avoids the problem, regarding body and mind as existing only in the eye of the beholder. But if we adopt Marcel's distinction it is clear that what confronts us is not a problem but a mystery. I feel a pain in my leg, but I cannot observe body and mind from the outside to see how they interact to cause the pain. I may speak of having a body and a mind, but body and mind are what I am.

Freedom and cause in human behaviour is similarly perplexing. Rogers claims he has observed people acting freely in therapy but decides that, as a scientist, he must regard human behaviour as caused. He concludes that there is no satisfactory reconciliation to the paradox. Fromm's recognition of free will is tempered by an awareness of its puzzling relation to determinism. Fromm stresses that humans are free, but at the same time he emphasizes the extent to which what people do is caused by society. Mead emphasizes that human beings are shaped by society but they can still freely choose to see the world differently because of the (unexplained) I. Kelly says that there is freedom and cause in what human beings do, and that these relate to our being able or unable to adopt alternative constructs; this explains nothing.

But the failure of theorists is understandable. Free choice is not like the spin of a coin, nor is it like chance. Free will must mean some special kind of cause is at work, and one we have no experience of outside the free-will situation. Scientific analysis of free-choice situations is not possible because we cannot stand outside such a situation and study it objectively. We are involved in our free (or caused) actions – they are part of us. Free will (and determinism) is not a problem but an insoluble mystery.

What was it in E. M. Forster's *A Passage to India* that so horrified Mrs Moore on that ill-fated expedition to the Marabar Caves? Beneath the emptiness Mrs Moore recoiled from, she sensed some evil presence in the world. Our theories provide objective accounts of bad and good, wrong and right, and of the moral element in personality. But when science turns bad or evil into an object we stand outside of, it is no longer the evil of our and Mrs Moore's experience. When evil, good, wrong, right are made objects of detached scientific inquiry, we gain invaluable insight and understanding but only at an abstract level. With therapy the situation is different. Therapists may well experience good, bad, evil, right, wrong in their empathy with clients in psychotherapy. But when they try to turn this experience into theory – be they Freud, Fromm, Rogers – the reality dissipates. What confronts us with the moral element in personality is again a mystery.

Marcel's idea of mystery accounts for other difficulties encountered in the study of personality, such as our relationship with nature. Fromm speaks of the human species as 'the freak of the universe'. It is certainly odd that we do not feel at home in the only home we have – Earth. We are part of nature, subject to its laws, to growth, decay and death; but at the same time we feel ourselves strangers on Earth, like ships in dry dock. We feel ourselves to be different in a way a chimpanzee does not. Fromm's statement that human beings are 'set apart while being a part' captures this and expresses what – in Marcel's sense – a mystery is. In examining my relationship with the natural world, I cannot get outside nature and myself since I am part of the natural world. Since I cannot make myself and my relationship with nature into objects for detached scientific inquiry, mystery confronts us again. In his late writings Freud expresses our strange relationship with nature through the life and death instincts. But these so-called instincts seem close to poetry, metaphors for our experience, not scientific explanation. Mysteries have no explanation.

Human social life might seem sufficiently down-to-earth for a scientific account to be possible. But the variety of psychological theories proposed suggests that the relation between the individual and society is more puzzling than at first appears. Freud regarded society as a place of conflict, a dog-eat-dog world where all are in competition to have their needs gratified. The result is an uneasy compromise, a marketplace truce with violence always just below the surface. Fromm, by contrast, regards human society as a co-operative enterprise which arises from a deep need we all have for others. Mead also sees society as co-operative and regards it as the stuff out of which human personality is made. But the optimism of social behaviourism has to be qualified. Our roles – female, daughter, wife, mother – are not only the building blocks of our identity but also the bars of our imprisonment in society. For Skinner, society is a structure of mutual reinforcement by reward and punishment.

Clearly, personality psychology has greater difficulty in giving an account of the relationship between the individual and society than might be expected. The difficulty arises because in human social life we have yet another situation we cannot analyse objectively from the outside. We are involved in society and what we are studying is ourselves and our relationships. What confronts us is again a mystery.

'"What is love," he said, with a shrug, "except another name for the use of positive reinforcement?"' Skinner adds little to this single-sentence account of human love in *Walden Two*, and most other theories have surprisingly little to say about such an important area of human experience. Freud relates love to instincts, in particular sexual needs, but in his account the loved-one seems little more than a means of satisfying these needs as a sex object. Even in Freudian sublimation, love originates only from the frustration of instincts and remains rooted in our self-centred bodies. Fromm seems to see love as a basic human need and speaks positively of love as an achievement of the productive character, but this explains nothing. In our experience of love we lose (and find) ourselves in another person, and the boundary between self and other becomes blurred. With human love we are back to something we cannot stand apart from and analyse from the outside. Love confronts us in personality as a mystery.

Creativity is another puzzle. Though people differ in the extent of their creativeness everyone is able to make something, whether sentences, dance steps, or rose gardens. Psychologists of language assert that children and adults constantly create sentences that have never been spoken before. Behaviourism, accounting for all behaviour in terms of reinforcement of random actions, has difficulty in accounting for the new. People appear most human when they are not completely predictable and say or do something new. Perhaps what we find tedious and lacking human-ness about politicians, trade-unionists, company directors and others who have party lines to follow is the predictability of what they have to say. They really are like programmed computers! Freud resorts again to the vague, all-purpose idea of sublimation to explain creativity. Rogers would refer just as vaguely to humans fulfilling their potential. Fromm emphasizes human creativity and relates it to freedom, and gives no explanation. But people being creative – Mozart composing *The Magic Flute*, a fitter improvising a technical solution, a child making up an original sentence, a dancer inventing a new step for the samba – are involved in what they create. The distinction between creator and what is created disappears in the act of creation. Once it exists as musical notation, a gadget, a sentence, a dance routine, it is an object separate from the subject who made it. But in the creating, the distinction disappears, and this means that creativity is not a problem but a mystery.

Freud and the neo-Freudians, behaviourism and social behaviourism, and even humanistic approaches break down personality into parts. This reductionism that goes with considering personality as a problem has resulted in much knowledge and insight. But the idea of there being parts to a person in the same way as there are parts to a car, is absurd. Once personality is regarded as a problem and is broken down, we have difficulty, as with Humpty-Dumpty, in putting the pieces together again.

Personality is not a problem to be solved by reducing it to parts, because personality is not something we each *have* but is what we each *are*. Personality is an irreducible mystery.

We pick up a long and well-researched biography of a pop-star and read about his difficult childhood, his stormy adolescence, the women in his life, his fondness for his son, the restless years of middle age. We put down the book, feeling that something crucial about him has escaped us. If a psychologist rewrites the biography in scientific terms, using Freud or Fromm or Rogers or whoever, the account will read differently but we are still left with a sense of not having quite got the man. The psychological account provides more scientific knowledge and may be intellectually more insightful, but the human being evades our and the biographer's grasp. Further research may add to our knowledge of the pop-star, his childhood, work and marriages, but the additional data and the insight they provide take us no further. In studying someone's personality scientifically, we arrive at a boundary to our knowledge.

There are two possible explanations. First, that the boundary is only temporary, since the objective understanding of personality is a difficult but not impossible problem that science will eventually solve. The six accounts we have looked at are first approximations in an approach which will eventually yield a grand theory to explain everything about people. The second explanation, and this is my own position, is that the boundary will always be there. Theories of personality give us perspectives on people and provide invaluable insight and knowledge, but they do not explain personality. They fail to provide a true understanding of people or even to capture what it is to be human. Even with the aid of an informed and enlightened common sense, the scientific approach to personality will fail because personality is a mystery. A drunk drops his wallet in a dark part of the road but insists on searching under the street-light. When asked about this, he says: 'The light is better here.' Whatever sympathy we may have for the drunk – at least you can see what you are doing under the light – we know he will find his wallet only if he gropes around in the dark where he dropped it. However bright the light of scientific analysis, the whole person is not to be found there.

In scientific inquiry we arrive at a boundary to our understanding of personality; but we do not come to a dead-end. In a short story by Albert Camus, a wife stands at her husband's side and stares out across the desert. She is obsessed by the distant horizon, as if something unknown, which she has searched for all her life, waits for her there. Later that night, leaving her husband asleep in bed, she returns to stare out across the desert into the darkness. Something mysterious in the night thrills and possesses her, and she cries out in ecstasy.

Human personality is like the horizon and always recedes before the advance of objective inquiry. No scientific explanation will be found. But in our attempt to grasp personality scientifically, we experience something strange. As we reach out and are confronted by boundaries, we are filled with wonder at human personality, and we seem to touch mystery.

EPILOGUE

His invisible nature has been glimpsed through His creatures.

St Paul: Romans, 1:20

It is time for the debunking to stop. Personality is too important
to be left entirely to the zoologists, the computer buffs, and
even to the psychologists. Whatever our humble origins in
evolution we are not just jumped-up apes, or computers. We
may not be good but we are extraordinary, and the analysis of
science has failed to explain us.

One odd feature of personality, reflected in our experience, is
an incomplete, unfinished quality. If, as the cliché says, we are
all looking for something, it is clear that by and large we do
not find it. We seem always to be in transit to a more fulfilled
and satisfying state of affairs, which we never arrive at. We are
not so much human beings as human becomings. Freud
regarded this as merely the gap between what our instincts want
and what they get, the conflict between the pleasure principle
and the reality principle. But we know – even if the politicians
do not – that, no matter how much society improves, our desire
for completion will never be satisfied by what human society
has to offer. Our personality appears to seek a satisfaction
possible only in a type of experience which is different from
that found in human life. Though the potential of the universe
may have reached a high point in personality, fulfilment has
not. Evolution seems to have played a nasty trick, bringing into
existence human beings vast in their desire and potential, but
minute in their fulfilment and satisfaction. If we are a freak of
the universe, we are an unfortunate freak.

In their attempts to provide understanding, our six scientific

171

theories have broken down personality into parts and looked inside. If we keep personality whole and look outside, might personality provide any understanding of the universe in which it emerged? Personality's mysterious whole might in some way replicate the universe from which it evolved, as a sort of microcosm. If this is so, what would it say about the universe? Scaled up, personality would suggest a universe which is free and caused, mind-full, moral, social, creative, natural but not only natural, even characterized in some way by love. Science says that the universe is impersonal and completely natural, and that these qualities of personality evolved quite by chance. But if personality is only natural, why has science failed to explain it? When we regard personality as a mystery and scale it up, we are nudged in the direction of an even greater mystery – a personal universe.

A puzzling feature of the universe in which humans emerged is that it can be understood, even if human beings themselves cannot. This troubled Einstein: 'The most incomprehensible thing about the universe is that it is comprehensible.' There are underlying laws and regularities in nature, and we can understand them. The human species is a freak of the universe which, for unexplained reasons, is able to understand the universe in which it evolved. This may be chance. The alternative possibility is that the laws and regularities of the universe are the product of Mind. The universe is a product of Mind traditionally called God, and we can understand its laws and regularities because we resemble this Mind.

Certain theories of personality assert that in a universe where everything is caused, there emerged, by chance and in some unexplained way, human beings whose actions are free. Other theories assert that human behaviour is completely caused. Informed and enlightened common sense says that what humans do is sometimes free, sometimes what they do is caused, and sometimes it is both – though how freedom and cause relate remains a puzzle. If personality is a microcosm of the universe, what does human freedom (and determinism) suggest about the universe in which personality emerged?

In the medieval religious debate about why God made the

world, Christian theologians asserted that God did so because of His loving nature. Does this mean, it was asked, that when God made the world He had no alternative but to do so because of His loving nature, and was therefore not free? No, replied the theologians, the world is both the result of God's free choice and the inevitable consequence of the goodness of His nature. God was completely free when He made the world but because of His loving nature He had no choice. This is the very paradox that Rogers and others assert about people. When we are completely free we can choose only what is right and good. When we are completely human and free what we choose – love as opposed to hate, compassion rather than contempt – is the result of our nature, and we have no choice. We are free and determined in the way that God was, and we are so because each of us is a microcosm of this God.

The six theories try to explain, or explain away, a moral element in personality. Human beings have a notion of right and wrong from a very early age, and children complain 'That's not fair!' before they can argue why. Our theories, though disagreeing on what this moral element is, do agree that human beings have a notion of right and wrong. All cultures have such a notion and differ only slightly in what they regard as right and wrong.

Common speech refers to this moral dimension in personality as conscience. We are conscious of this conscience and are aware of it speaking to us. Conscience tells us what we 'ought' and 'ought not' do, and informs us if what we do is right or wrong. Conscience praises, encourages, blames, threatens, conveys approval or criticism, and does this in the way a person would. Conscience is like someone there expecting something of us, and what we hear is a voice, a voice in a relationship. What we hear is not something but Someone. There is a moral element in personality because a Moral Being is at the origin of the universe from which personality emerged. Another possibility is that moral conscience in human beings evolved quite by chance, but as yet there is no satisfactory description of how this happened. And the accounts of this moral dimension which our six theories provide seem inadequate.

If personality and its odd features are the product of chance in a meaningless material universe, personality can have nothing to say about this universe. We would then expect science eventually to explain personality. But human beings may be as they are, and have such odd features, because the universe they evolved from is not merely material and does have meaning. Evolution may have ended with human personality because it began from Personality. Human beings have minds . . . are free in a strange, caused way . . . are morally concerned . . . part of but apart from the natural world . . . capable of love, relationships and creativity . . . because of the Personal nature of the universe from which they emerged. Personality's desire and potential, its lack of fulfilment and the awareness that nothing in human experience can fully satisfy, point to the one possibility that would fulfil such a creature. The mystery of personality points to a personal God.

'Thrown into the world I become a puzzle to myself'; scientific theory has failed to find a solution to St Augustine's puzzle. But in examining and analysing personality scientifically, we confront boundaries and encounter a mystery. Religion has traditionally taught that human beings are made in the image of God. This would explain why we have difficulty in understanding personality. It would explain why, in our attempt to understand personality, we often experience wonder and awe. If human beings are made in God's image it would explain why – at the boundaries of our scientific knowing of human personality – we sometimes sense beyond the mystery of human personality a much greater Mystery.

SOURCES

The following are the main sources for each chapter, and readers will find some of the books listed interesting and readable. But since a number of these books are technical, advanced or rather specialized, a second list of Suggestions for Further Reading, with comments on each text, is added.

Chapter 2. Sigmund Freud (1856–1939)

SIGMUND FREUD, *The Interpretation of Dreams*, 1900. Complete Psychological Works, vol. 5, Hogarth Press.

New Introductory Lectures on Psycho-Analysis, 1933. Complete Works, vol. 22, Hogarth Press.

An Outline of Psycho-Analysis, 1940. Complete Works, vol. 23, Hogarth Press.

Leonardo da Vinci, 1910. Complete Works, vol. 11, Hogarth Press.

Parapraxes, 1916. Complete Works, vol. 15, Hogarth Press.

Civilisation and its Discontents, Hogarth Press, 1930.

Chapter 3. B. F. Skinner (1904–   )

B. F. SKINNER, *Beyond Freedom and Dignity*, Penguin, 1973.

Walden Two, Macmillan, 1948.

Science and Human Behaviour, Collier-Macmillan, London; Free Press, New York; 1953.

Chapter 4. Carl Rogers (1902–87)

CARL ROGERS, *On Becoming a Person*, Constable, 1961.

A Way of Being, Houghton Mifflin, 1980.

Freedom to Learn for the 80's, Charles E. Merrill Publishing Co., 1983.

'A Note on "The Nature of Man"', *Journal of Counselling Psychology*, 1957, 4:3.

Chapter 5. Erich Fromm (1900–80)

ERICH FROMM, *The Fear of Freedom*, Routledge & Kegan Paul, 1942. (Published in the US as *Escape from Freedom*, New York, Rinehart, 1941.)

Man for Himself, Routledge & Kegan Paul, 1949.

To have or to be?, Jonathan Cape, 1976.

The Heart of Man, Routledge & Kegan Paul, 1964.

The Anatomy of Human Destructiveness, Penguin, 1977. (Published in the US by Holt, Rinehart & Winston, 1973.)

Chapter 6. G. H. Mead (1863–1931)

GEORGE HERBERT MEAD, *Mind, Self and Society*, University of Chicago Press, 1934.

The Individual and the Social Self, in *Unpublished Work of George Herbert Mead*, ed. David L. Miller, University of Chicago Press, 1982.

M. BANTON, *Roles*, Tavistock, 1965.

Chapter 7. George Kelly (1905–67)

GEORGE KELLY, *The Psychology of Personal Constructs*, vols 1 & 2, W. W. Norton & Co., 1955.

Chapter 8.

GABRIEL MARCEL, *The Philosophy of Existence*, Harvill Press, 1949.

Being and Having, Harper & Row, 1965.

KARL JASPERS, *Way to Wisdom*, Yale University Press, 1954.

Philosophy of Existence, Basil Blackwell, 1971.

SUGGESTIONS FOR FURTHER READING

Chapter 1. The Puzzle

JEROME A. SHAFFER, *Philosophy of Mind*, Prentice-Hall, Englewood Cliffs, 1968. This is an excellent introduction to mind, the person, consciousness, body–mind and similar areas.

JOHN SEARLE, *Minds, Brain and Science*, BBC, 1984. This is the Reith Lecture given by a leading American philosopher, the Professor of Philosophy at University of California. In 100 pages such topics as the mind–body problem, whether computers can think, cognitive science and the freedom of the will are explored in a readable style.

KARL R. POPPER and JOHN C. ECCLES, *The Self and its Brain: An Argument for Interactionism*, Springer International, 1977. A long, fascinating book in which an outstanding philosopher of science and an eminent brain scientist explore the question of mind, and in particular its relation to body. To the surprise of many, they come down on the side of the dualist interactionist position – mental states are something different from the material brain they interact with.

GEOFFREY MADELL, *The Identity of the Self*, Edinburgh University Press, 1981. This brilliant little book questions the view of behaviourists and others that the I of personal identity is an illusion or can be reduced to something else. It asserts the academically unpopular but common-sense position that the I is real.

GEOFFREY MADELL, *Mind and Materialism*, Edinburgh University Press, 1988. This is a fascinating but very difficult book, aimed mainly at other philosophers. It argues the view, unpopular with most modern philosophers and psychologists, that materialist explanations of mind cannot succeed. The author contends that any solution to the body–mind problem will have to take into account Descartes' idea of mind as non-material and different from body.

D. J. O'CONNOR, *Free Will*, Macmillan, 1972. A short, clear, interesting and readable introduction to the free will and determinism debate.

JENIFER TRUSTED, *Free Will and Responsibility*, Oxford University Press, 1984. A book outlining the issues and arguing for the reality of free will. No prior knowledge of philosophy is required, but the book is possibly more suited to those particularly interested in the area.

W. K. FRANKENA, *Ethics*, Prentice-Hall Inc., 2nd edn, 1973. This is a first-rate short introduction to philosophical thought about moral rules, the study of which moral rules actually guide human beings, and the attempt to establish which rules ought to guide human behaviour.

MARY MIDGLEY, *Wickedness: a philosophical essay*, Routledge & Kegan Paul, 1984 (now an ARK paperback). An interesting, wide-ranging discussion of many issues related to 'bad' human behaviour. Free will, morality, aggression, the issue of what is innate or learnt and internal or external in human behaviour, and the question of human nature generally, are all examined.

O. A. JOHNSON, *Ethics: Selections from Classical and Contemporary Writers*, Holt, Rinehart & Winston, 5th edn, 1984. A source book of different writings for those particularly interested in ethics.

C. S. LEWIS, *The Abolition of Man*, Collins Fount Paperbacks, 1982 (first published 1943). In this short and stimulating book of 60 pages, Lewis is defending what might be called a common-sense position in ethics, the unfashionable Natural Law theory. It is the view that certain values and actions are right and that certain other values and actions are wrong – it is just part of our nature that they are. He then provides a list of what constitutes this Natural Law in various traditions.

R. NORMAN, *The Moral Philosophers: An Introduction to*

Ethics, Clarendon Press, Oxford, 1983. This clear and readable introduction to ethics is structured in terms of the positions of different philosophers and thinkers such as Plato, J. S. Mill and Freud.

E. R. VALENTINE, *Conceptual Issues in Psychology*, George Allen & Unwin, 1982. An interesting book pitched at a moderate level of difficulty, which covers a variety of topics; among them are consciousness, body–mind, free will and determinism, explanations in terms of purpose, and the nature of scientific theory.

JAY N. EACKER, *Problems of Philosophy and Psychology*, Nelson-Hall, Chicago, 1975. An interesting book which presents in a clear way a variety of philosophical issues relating to psychology, such as body–mind, freedom and fact-value.

DANIEL N. ROBINSON, *Philosophy of Psychology*, Columbia University Press, New York, 1985. An interesting book which covers free will and determinism, reductionist nothing-but explanations, the attempts of psychology to deal with mind, and which also says something on ethics and psychology. Like nearly all writing in this area of the philosophy of psychology, the book assumes the materialist position – that only the physical exists.

Chapter 2. Freud's Psycho-analysis

PAUL KLINE, *Fact and Fantasy in Freudian Theory*, Methuen, 1972. Written by a psychologist sympathetic to psychoanalytic theory, this academic text investigates what support Freudian theory is given by scientific research. More suitable for those with a special interest in the area.

PAUL KLINE, *Psychology and Freudian Theory: An introduction*, Methuen, 1984. This shorter text is less academic and easier to read than the earlier book. It gives a clear account of Freud's ideas, besides exploring the evidence for and the implications of Freudian thought.

STEVEN MARCUS, *Freud and the Culture of Psychoanalysis*, Allen & Unwin, 1984. Written by the Professor of English and Comparative Literature at Columbia University, the book is concerned with how Freud's ideas developed within a specific historical and cultural situation. This is a text more suitable for those with a particular interest in the area.

H. J. EYSENCK, *Decline and Fall of the Freudian Empire*, Penguin, 1985. The book makes no bones about its intentions: it attempts to expose what it sees as the limitations, contradictions and falsity of Freudian theory and psycho-analytic practice. It is clear and readable.

PERRY MEISEL, ed., *Freud: A collection of critical essays*, Prentice-Hall Inc., 1981. A variety of interesting essays relating Freudian ideas to subjects such as art, literature and dreams. Among the contributors are W. H. Auden, Thomas Mann and Leonard Woolf.

S. FISHER and R. P. GREENBERG, *The Scientific Credibility of Freud's Theories and Therapy*, 1977, Basic Books, New York, and Harvester Press, Sussex. A substantial text which presents the bulk of Freudian ideas and examines what evidence there is to support them. This is more a book for the advanced student.

Chapter 3. Behaviourism

STEPHEN WALKER, *Learning Theory and Behaviour Modification*, Methuen, 1984. The book provides a clear account of behaviour therapy and the ideas that underpin it, largely those of behaviourism.

A. BANDURA, *Social Learning Theory*, Prentice-Hall Inc., 1977. A high-level academic text which attempts to provide a theoretical framework in the area. Cognitive psychology has now become central to psychology, and this book attempts to introduce cognitive factors like expectancy into the behaviourist framework.

A. BANDURA, *Aggression: a social learning analysis*, Prentice-Hall Inc., 1973. A specialized academic text which uses behaviourist social learning theory to explain different types of aggressive behaviour. It examines the implications of a behaviourist social learning explanation for reducing aggression.

FINLEY CARPENTER, *The Skinner Primer: Behind Freedom and Dignity*, Collier Macmillan and Free Press, 1974. The book is concerned with Skinner's contention in *Beyond Freedom and Dignity* that human beings are not free. The author surveys Skinner's behaviourism before examining Skinner's account of freedom, and argues for the reality of a certain type of freedom.

HARVEY WHEELER, ed., *Beyond the Punitive Society. Operant Conditioning: Social and Political Aspects*, W. H. Freeman & Co., San Francisco, 1973. This is a varied collection of interesting articles, in part a response to Skinner's *Beyond Freedom and Dignity*.

Chapter 4. Carl Rogers

The three books by Rogers listed above under Sources are all very readable: *On Becoming a Person*, *A Way of Being*, *Freedom to Learn for the 80's*. But most of what Rogers has written is readable.

R. I. EVANS, *Carl Rogers: the Man and his Ideas*, E. P. Dutton, New York, 1975. The book contains an introduction to Rogers' ideas as well as his 'debate' with Skinner. The main part of the text is an edited transcript of a dialogue in which Evans explores with Rogers his thinking on a wide variety of topics. The book concludes with two articles by Rogers.

Chapter 5. Erich Fromm

The five books by Fromm listed above under Sources are very readable, and Fromm always writes with style and grace.

RAINER FUNK, *Erich Fromm: The Courage to be Human*, Continuum, New York, 1982. This is a comprehensive, clear and sympathetic account of Fromm's work. The book is for the reader particularly interested in Fromm.

JOHN H. SCHAAR, *Escape from Authority: the Perspectives of Erich Fromm*, Basic Books, 1961. The book is an intelligent and powerful attack on Fromm's ideas.

Chapter 6. Role theory and Mead's symbolic interactionism

PETER L. BERGER, *Invitation to Sociology: a humanistic perspective*, Penguin, 1963. Old, but this remains a first-rate book which is constantly being reprinted. It presents a very readable account of those perspectives in social science which emphasize that personality is made by society.

J. C. MANIS and B. N. MELTZER, eds, *Symbolic Interaction*, Allyn & Bacon Inc., 3rd edn, 1978. Earlier editions (1967, 1972) are also useful. Aimed at the specialist, the book provides a good collection of articles for the more academic reader particularly interested in the area. Meltzer's article, 'Mead's Social Psychology', is excellent.

PAUL ROCK, *The Making of Symbolic Interactionism*, Macmillan Press, 1979. A good academic study of symbolic interactionism, placing it in context. Comprehensive but written at a high level of abstraction and more for the academic reader.

Chapter 7. George Kelly's construct theory

D. BANNISTER and F. FRANSELLA, *Inquiring Man: The Psychology of Personal Constructs*, Croom Helm, 3rd edn, 1986. This, and the earlier editions published by Penguin, are probably the best and most readable introductions to construct theory. The 1986 edition considers the applications of Kelly's ideas and how they are becoming central to psychology.

D. BANNISTER, ed., *New Perspectives in Personal Construct Theory*, Academic Press/Harcourt Brace Jovanovich, 1977. This is an excellent collection of intelligent and interesting essays, but more suited for the reader already well acquainted with Kelly's thought.

J. R. ADAMS-WEBBER, *Personal Construct Theory: Concepts and Applications*, John Wiley & Sons, 1979. This is a knowledgeable book which explores research in construct theory and examines the theory's development. A comprehensive account, more for the academic reader particularly interested in the area.

INDEX

FOR THE BEST IN PAPERBACKS, LOOK FOR THE ⬤

Political Ideas David Thomson (ed.)

From Machiavelli to Marx – a stimulating and informative introduction to the last 500 years of European political thinkers and political thought.

On Revolution Hannah Arendt

Arendt's classic analysis of a relatively recent political phenomenon examines the underlying principles common to all revolutions, and the evolution of revolutionary theory and practice. 'Never dull, enormously erudite, always imaginative' – *Sunday Times*

The Apartheid Handbook Roger Omond

The facts behind the headlines: the essential hard information about how apartheid actually works from day to day.

The Social Construction of Reality Peter Berger and Thomas Luckmann

Concerned with the sociology of 'everything that passes for knowledge in society' and particularly with that which passes for common sense, this is 'a serious, open-minded book, upon a serious subject' – *Listener*

The Care of the Self Michel Foucault
The History of Sexuality Vol 3

Foucault examines the transformation of sexual discourse from the Hellenistic to the Roman world in an inquiry which 'bristles with provocative insights into the tangled liaison of sex and self' – *The Times Higher Educational Supplement*

A Fate Worse than Debt Susan George

How did Third World countries accumulate a staggering trillion dollars' worth of debt? Who really shoulders the burden of reimbursement? How should we deal with the debt crisis? Susan George answers these questions with the solid evidence and verve familiar to readers of *How the Other Half Dies*.

I: The Philosophy and Psychology of Personal Identity   Jonathan Glover

From cases of split brains and multiple personalities to the importance of memory and recognition by others, the author of *Causing Death and Saving Lives* tackles the vexed questions of personal identity. 'Fascinating ... the ideas which Glover pours forth in profusion deserve more detailed consideration' – Anthony Storr

Minds, Brains and Science   John Searle

Based on Professor Searle's acclaimed series of Reith Lectures, *Minds, Brains and Science* is 'punchy and engaging ... a timely exposé of those woolly-minded computer-lovers who believe that computers can think, and indeed that the human mind is just a biological computer' – *The Times Literary Supplement*

Ethics   Inventing Right and Wrong   J. L. Mackie

Widely used as a text, Mackie's complete and clear treatise on moral theory deals with the status and content of ethics, sketches a practical moral system and examines the frontiers at which ethics touches psychology, theology, law and politics.

The Penguin History of Western Philosophy   D. W. Hamlyn

'Well-crafted and readable ... neither laden with footnotes nor weighed down with technical language ... a general guide to three millennia of philosophizing in the West' – *The Times Literary Supplement*

Science and Philosophy: Past and Present   Derek Gjertsen

Philosophy and science, once intimately connected, are today often seen as widely different disciplines. Ranging from Aristotle to Einstein, from quantum theory to renaissance magic, Confucius and parapsychology, this penetrating and original study shows such a view to be both naive and ill-informed.

The Problem of Knowledge   A. J. Ayer

How do you *know* that this is a book? How do you *know* that you know? In *The Problem of Knowledge* A. J. Ayer presented the sceptic's arguments as forcefully as possible, investigating the extent to which they can be met. 'Thorough ... penetrating, vigorous ... readable and manageable' – *Spectator*

PENGUIN PSYCHOLOGY

Introduction to Jung's Psychology   Frieda Fordham

'She has delivered a fair and simple account of the main aspects of my psychological work. I am indebted to her for this admirable piece of work' – C. G. Jung in the Foreword

Child Care and the Growth of Love   John Bowlby

His classic 'summary of evidence of the effects upon children of lack of personal attention … it presents to administrators, social workers, teachers and doctors a reminder of the significance of the family' – *The Times*

The Anatomy of Human Destructiveness   Erich Fromm

What makes men kill? How can we explain man's lust for cruelty and destruction? 'If any single book could bring mankind to its senses, this book might qualify for that miracle' – Lewis Mumford

Sanity, Madness and the Family   R. D. Laing and A. Esterson

Schizophrenia: fact or fiction? Certainly not fact, according to the authors of this controversial book. Suggesting that some forms of madness may be largely social creations, *Sanity, Madness and the Family* demands to be taken very seriously indeed.

The Social Psychology of Work   Michael Argyle

Both popular and scholarly, Michael Argyle's classic account of the social factors influencing our experience of work examines every area of working life – and throws constructive light on potential problems.

Check Your Own I.Q.   H. J. Eysenck

The sequel to his controversial bestseller, containing five new standard (omnibus) tests and three specifically designed tests for verbal, numerical and visual–spatial ability.

FOR THE BEST IN PAPERBACKS, LOOK FOR THE 🐧

PENGUIN PSYCHOLOGY

Psychoanalysis and Feminism   Juliet Mitchell

'Juliet Mitchell has risked accusations of apostasy from her fellow feminists. Her book not only challenges orthodox feminism, however; it defies the conventions of social thought in the English-speaking countries ... a brave and important book' – *New York Review of Books*

Helping Troubled Children   Michael Rutter

Written by a leading practitioner and researcher in child psychiatry, a full and clear account of the many problems encountered by young school-age children – development, emotional disorders, underachievement – and how they can be given help.

The Divided Self   R. D. Laing

A study that makes all other works I have read on schizophrenia seem fragmentary ... The author brings, through his vision and perception, that particular touch of genius which causes one to say "Yes, I have always known that, why have I never thought of it before?"' – *Journal of Analytical Psychology*

The Origins of Religion   Sigmund Freud

The thirteenth volume in the *Penguin Freud Library* contains Freud's views on the subject of religious belief – including *Totem and Taboo*, regarded by Freud as his best-written work.

The Informed Heart   Bruno Bettelheim

Bettelheim draws on his experience in concentration camps to illuminate the dangers inherent in all mass societies in this profound and moving masterpiece.

Introducing Social Psychology   Henri Tajfel and Colin Fraser (eds.)

From evolutionary changes to the social influence processes in a given group, a distinguished team of contributors demonstrate how our interaction with others and our views of the social world shape and modify much of what we do.